The First People *of the* Cape

A look at their history and the impact of colonialism
on the Cape's indigenous people

The First People of the Cape

A look at their history and the impact of colonialism on the Cape's indigenous people

Alan Mountain

dp **davidphilip**

First published 2003 by David Philip Publishers,
an imprint of New Africa Books (Pty) Ltd, 99 Garfield Road,
Claremont, 7700, South Africa

ISBN 0-86486-623-2

Text and photographs © 2003 Alan Mountain

All rights reserved. No part of this publication may be reproduced, stored in a retrieval system, or transmitted in any form or by any means, electronic, mechanical, photocopying, recording or otherwise, without the prior written permission of the publishers.

Additional photographs by Graham Avery / Iziko: South African Museum (p. 13); Paul Weinberg / South Photographs (pp. 10, 23); Pieter Jolly (pp. 38, 39, 79); National Library of South Africa (pp. 68, 70, 71, 72)

Back cover photograph and rock art image on p. 22 from *Rock Paintings of South Africa: Revealing a Legacy* by Stephen Townley Bassett (Cape Town: David Philip Publishers, 2001)

Cover design and typography by *Peter Bosman*
Design and typesetting by *Lyndall du Toit*
Cartography by *John Hall*
Editing by *Roelien Theron*
Reproduction by House of Colours, Cape Town
Printed and bound by CTP Book Printers,
Duminy Street, Parow, Cape Town, South Africa

Contents

Preface 7
Acknowledgements 9

CHAPTER 1 AFRICA'S EARLIEST PEOPLE: THE EVOLUTION OF MODERN HUMANS 10
The Earlier Stone Age: The first toolmakers 10
The Middle Stone Age: The emergence of modern humans 14
The Later Stone Age: An age of more precise innovation 16

Information boxes
What is the Stone Age? 11
Klasies River Main Site 14
Blombos Cave 15
Middens – Relics of ancient times 18
Matjes River Rock Shelter 20

CHAPTER 2 THE SAN: STONE AGE PEOPLE OF THE CAPE 22
A close bond with the land 25
Conflict with the colonists 26
Genocide becomes an option 29
The British arrive at the Cape 31
A change of heart in the north-east 33
The north-western frontier remains recalcitrant 35
The Cape San are no more 36

Information boxes
A note on nomenclature: What's in a name? 23
Trekboer architecture 32
San rock art in the Western Cape 38

CONTENTS

CHAPTER 3 THE KHOEKHOEN: FIRST HERDERS OF THE CAPE — 40
The move southwards — 41
A pastoralist way of life — 42
A meeting of two different worlds — 46
The Dutch establish a base at the Cape — 47
Conflict erupts — 50
Status of the Khoekhoen — 52
An ambivalent relationship — 53
The English occupy the Cape — 56

Information boxes
Boomplaas Cave — 43
A home rooted in tradition — 45
Autshumato and the *Strandlopers* — 50
Krotoa — 51
Smallpox and Khoekhoe labour — 53
Mission stations – Places of refuge for the landless — 59

CHAPTER 4 THE KHOE-SAN: DIVISION AND DEMOCRACY IN THE NINETEENTH AND TWENTIETH CENTURIES — 62
Representative government — 65
The looming crisis — 67
A precarious honeymoon and painful divorce — 70
The advent of democracy — 73

Information boxes
A note on nomenclature: Who are the coloured people? — 64
Abdullah Abdurahman and the African Political Organisation — 68

CHAPTER 5 THE KHOE-SAN: DIGNITY SELF-WORTH AND ASPIRATIONS — 74
Early science and racial superiority — 75
Rebuilding the past — 79
Promoting Khoe-San interests — 80
An international perspective — 86
Unity in diversity — 86

Information boxes
The return of Sarah Bartmann — 78
The Griqua Ratelgat Development Trust Project — 81
Can the Griqua claim first people status? — 83
!Khwa ttu San Culture and Education Centre — 85
A brief history of the Griqua — 88

NOTES — 100

PREFACE

THIS BOOK PROVIDES an overview of the fascinating history of both the San hunter-gatherers and the Khoekhoe herders in the Western Cape – the first inhabitants of this region. It also argues that the recognition of the rights of these first people and the positive implications this could have for sustainable development and empowerment are long overdue.

Archaeological evidence shows that the Khoekhoen and the San are people of great antiquity – indeed the San have the oldest genetic stock of contemporary humanity. Their presence in South Africa can be traced back over many thousands of years – antedating both the arrival of Bantu-speaking immigrants and European colonists. The Khoekhoen are immigrants who arrived in the Western Cape about 2 000 years ago and co-existed with the San. Bantu-speaking farmers were present south of the Limpopo probably from the second or third century onwards, but did not settle in the south-western Cape as it is a winter rainfall area and they only had summer rainfall crops. European colonisation began in the Cape in the 1600s and its long-term effects were devastating for the San and the Khoekhoen.

Colonialism almost wiped out both the San and Khoekhoen as coherent ethnic entities in the Cape. The San suffered genocide, disease and forced emigration, whereas the Khoekhoen were affected by dispossession, disease and acculturation. Only isolated pockets of 'ethnically pure' indigenous people remain – some San who live mainly in Namibia and Botswana and some Khoekhoen who live mainly in Namaqualand. Collectively, however, their legacy forms a major constituent of the Western Cape's coloured population, the majority population group in the province today.

The psychological effects of colonial domination were as devastating as the physical effects. Domination by one group over another is a double-edged sword. On the one side it cuts away the indigenous social institutions which provide the foundation upon which social continuity and credibility are built. The removal of these institutions invariably results in instability, a lack of self-esteem, and dependency on others. The other side of the sword severs through compassion, concern and understanding, encouraging the dominators to feel indifference or contempt and a sense of inherent superiority towards the dominated. Apartheid policies reinforced the social, economic and political inequities bequeathed by the colonial period. Notwithstanding the many dramatic changes since 1994, South Africa still faces a difficult challenge: it must heal

PREFACE

the wounds the sword of domination has inflicted, in order to prevent them from continuing to fester. Despite a decade of democracy, many descendants of the Cape's first people, a minority in a majoritarian society, still carry the burdens of disempowerment and alienation.

What then is the remedy for this legacy of disempowerment and alienation left by colonialism and its successor, apartheid? We need to begin by recognising the rights of indigenous people. The United Nations proclaimed the decade 1995–2004 as the International Decade of the World's Indigenous Peoples. The main objective of this decade is the strengthening of international cooperation for the solution of problems faced by indigenous people in such areas as human rights, the environment, development, health, culture and education. The International Labour Organization has also done valuable work in promoting the concept of indigenous rights, which is discussed further in Chapter 5.

The United Nations has established several criteria to evaluate claims to indigenous rights. These include indigenous people's retention of social, cultural, economic and political characteristics that are distinct from those of the dominant societies in which they live; a historical and close relationship to the land as well as the sustainable use of natural resources for subsistence; a bloodline claim to a specific territory; and a history of the political, social and economic marginalisation of indigenous people by the dominant immigrants.

However, the recognition of rights needs to be accompanied by action towards realising those rights, as this will provide opportunities for sustainable development and growth. A start has been made with the implementation of a number of projects intended to give effect to this process, some of which are described in this book. Their success and those of similar projects and processes are of crucial importance, especially since it is capacity-building and the substantive empowerment that it engenders that will provide a lasting balm to the wounds inflicted by the double-edged sword of domination. There is a risk, however, as failure will serve to reaffirm the feelings of inadequacy on the one hand and the stereotype of contempt on the other, thereby adding considerably to the already heavy costs of social dysfunction.

ACKNOWLEDGEMENTS

A BOOK OF this nature requires the assistance of many people and institutions. Sometimes the support I received was direct and tangible and sometimes it was instructional or inspirational – whatever its form, I am grateful to all who played a part in helping me to put this book together. In particular, I would like to mention Hilary Deacon, a former professor of archaeology at Stellenbosch University, who gave unstintingly of his time and put me on the path of understanding the Cape's exciting archaeology. His generous assistance in the supply of research material saved me much wandering in the wilderness and for this I am most grateful. I am indebted to Mary Leslie for the advice she gave me on the importance of archaeology in understanding the peopling of southern Africa. In acknowledging the assistance I received from experts, I wish to make it absolutely clear that all interpretation is mine and therefore any omissions or errors are also mine.

I wish to thank His Excellency Paramount Chief Andrew Stockenstrom Le Fleur II for the gracious hospitality he extended to me at Kranshoek and for the moving reception at the Pioneers Monument, where I had the opportunity to listen to his personal choir and to meet some of the Elders and members of the Griqua community. My gratitude goes to David Cloete who made this possible. I would especially like to thank Cecil Le Fleur, chairman of the Griqua National Council of South Africa, for his insights into Griqua thinking and for sharing his knowledge of Griqua history. I am grateful to Chief Joseph Little for broadening my understanding of Khoekhoe history. My thanks go to Roderick Williams who, on short notice, provided me with extensive documentation from the Griqua archives.

To the many descendants of the Khoe-San who shared their views and perspectives, I owe the entire reason for writing this book. To them – too numerous to mention individually – I shall always be indebted.

I would like to express my gratitude to George Hofmeyr of the former National Monuments Council for his encouragement and support at the commencement of this project. I am also most grateful to Mrs Pumla Madiba, chief executive officer of the South African Heritage Resources Agency, and her staff for making the Agency's files, records and library available to me without restriction. I was fortunate to have worked with Jane Ayres who never tired of locating relevant material for me. My thanks also go to Benedict Rodgers for his cheerful help in finding files for me. David Hart's wise counsel and valued support are much appreciated.

My gratitude also goes to the John and Charles Bell Heritage Trust and the Brenthurst Press for their generous permission to reproduce illustrations from their respective collections.

I would like to thank Roelien Theron, the book's indefatigable editor, and Lyndall du Toit, whose book design skills I have always admired, for their dedicated and talented contributions.

Finally, my heartfelt thanks go to my wife, Jenny, for putting up with my long periods of absence – either away from home or preoccupied in my office.

CHAPTER 1

Africa's earliest people

THE EVOLUTION OF MODERN HUMANS

The earliest representatives of humankind, the australopithecines or 'southern apemen', once inhabited the southern regions of the African continent. Indeed, the famous Sterkfontein Valley – the Cradle of Humankind – has yielded important evidence of the origins of modern humans. Declared a World Heritage Site in 1999, the valley near Krugersdorp in Gauteng is one of the richest sources of australopithecine fossils yet found in the world and has yielded over half the known individuals of the genera *Australopithecus* and *Paranthropus*. About 2.5 million years ago these two genera followed separate evolutionary paths: while the paranthropines became extinct, the australopithecines evolved into modern humans (*Homo sapiens sapiens*). In the lineage of *Homo*, various species are recognised in an evolutionary line leading to *Homo sapiens sapiens*.

THE EARLIER STONE AGE: THE FIRST TOOLMAKERS

The qualification for the status of *Homo* is the ability to shape tools out of stone. Stone tool-making in Africa began some 2.5 million years ago, marking the beginning of the archaeology period described as the Earlier Stone Age. The oldest evidence of tool-making in the world is at Gona in the Awash Valley in Ethiopia where some 3 000 well-

WHAT IS THE STONE AGE?

The division of the Stone Age into Earlier, Middle and Later Stone Ages was first proposed by archaeologist John Hilary Goodwin in the 1929 article 'Stone Age cultures of South Africa', written in collaboration with Peter van Riet Lowe and published in the *Annals of the South African Museum*. Although Goodwin and Van Riet Lowe could not provide precise estimates of the time ranges of these stages, modern dating methods have since been used to establish more accurate dating divisions. The Earlier Stone Age, approximately 2.5 million to 250 000 years ago, is characterised by large bifacial (flaked on both faces) artefacts, with the distinctive handaxes being the most pervasive form. The Middle Stone Age, which ended between 30 000 and 22 000 years ago, is characterised by the skilful preparation of cores (blocks of stone) to produce regular triangular or parallel-sided flakes, some of which were mounted on handles. The transition to the Later Stone Age began about 22 000 years ago, and provided the link with historical times. This period is characterised by the production of small stone tools (microliths) and blades (used as knives and arrowheads). Important features of the Later Stone Age are the practices of burial and rock art.[1]

made artefacts, dated to 2.5 million years ago, have been found. At Hadar, not far from Gona, artefacts that are approximately 2.3 million years old have been discovered. Early examples of stone tools have also been uncovered in the rocky Olduvai Gorge in Tanzania. These were produced about 1.8 million years ago. Known as the Oldowan artefacts, these rudimentary implements are considered by archaeologists to represent 'a starter-level stone toolkit that reveals little control over design, other than reducing cores to flakes.'[2] The removal of flakes from a stone core was the minimum requirement for the stone to function as a tool. The Oldowan technology that created these basic tools was used for the first million years of the Earlier Stone Age. Tools such as those found in the Olduvai Gorge were uncovered at various sites along the Rift Valley from Tanzania to Ethiopia and in Malawi. In South Africa, they were excavated at the Sterkfontein Caves and at Swartkrans and recovered from gravel deposits along the Vaal River.

Artefacts – Archaeologists' evidence

Stone tools, bits of pottery, bones, bored stones and, in some cases, organic matter provide the evidence on which archaeologists base their understanding of our prehistoric past. The earliest of these artefacts date back to about 2.5 million years, the beginning of the Earlier Stone Age. It is generally accepted that the appearance of the first flaked stone tools correlates with the emergence of the first true humans, our early ancestors. Potsherds – the remains of earthenware pottery – are a more recent addition to the archaeological record. Most of the pottery fragments found at archaeological sites in South Africa date back to within the last 2 000 years.

About 1.4 million years ago in Africa, and later in Asia and Europe, these early stone tools were developed into a more refined set of tools known as bifaces – large, shaped cores, flaked on both faces according to a pattern. Classified as handaxes and cleavers, these implements were pear- or almond-shaped. They tended to be broader at the base than they were thick and ranged in length from 100 to 200 millimetres. The change from simply flaking a core to now shaping that core to make it into a more efficient tool marked the introduction of style and the making of choices about what and how to shape things. Making choices is a function of the mind; and the emergence of new tools involving this ability marked the transition from proto-human behaviour to human behaviour.

Tools of the Earlier Stone Age were first studied in South Africa by Louis Albert Péringuey, a former director of the South African Museum. While working in Stellenbosch in 1899, Péringuey inspected a quarry site where he chanced upon a bifacial stone tool in a road-maker's borrow pit. Encouraged by the find, he conducted a more detailed search locally as well as in the greater Stellenbosch area. After careful analysis of his finds, he concluded that they were about 250 000 years old – at least as ancient as some of the European tools he had compared them with. He announced his finding in a paper, 'Notes on stone implements of Palaeolithic (Old Stone Age) type found at Stellenbosch and vicinity', delivered to the South African Philosophical Society in August 1900. The paper evoked considerable interest, especially since it suggested that humans had a longer history of living in Africa than had previously been thought to be the case. What seemed a revolutionary suggestion at the time has since been validated by modern dating methods, and today it is widely accepted that Péringuey's almond-shaped stone implements are at least half a million years old.

Péringuey's finds led to the use of the term 'Stellenbosch Culture' to describe the bifacial tools of the Earlier Stone Age. However, it has since been replaced by the international term 'Acheulian', derived from the archaeological site of St Acheul in France.

Stellenbosch Archaeological Reserve

Dr Louis Péringuey's discovery of stone artefacts in Stellenbosch in 1899 made him the first researcher to establish the immense antiquity of the Stone Age people who inhabited southern Africa. His findings evoked considerable controversy in the late nineteenth century when the revolutionary thought that people had lived in Africa for at least as long as they had in Europe was difficult for some European archaeologists to accept. Since Péringuey's discovery in Stellenbosch, a number of sites have been found in southern Africa containing an astonishing collection of Earlier Stone Age artefacts. The place where Péringuey found his first stone tool is commemorated in a small archaeological reserve marked by this memorial. The Stellenbosch Archaeological Reserve is a provincial heritage site.

Fossil footprints in the sands of time

Over 117 000 years ago an anatomically modern person walked across a damp sand dune next to Langebaan Lagoon north-west of modern-day Cape Town, leaving behind a trail of footprints. In due course, the footprints were covered by sand and became fossilised as the dune gradually hardened into rock. They were discovered in 1995 and are thought to have been made by a woman. Their significance lies in their age: scientists believe they were formed at a time – between 200 000 and 100 000 years ago – when the first modern humans evolved, making them the oldest modern human footprints yet discovered. The footprints corroborate evidence found at Klasies River Mouth on the Tsitsikamma coast and at Border Cave in the Lebombo Mountains, showing that anatomically modern humans were present in southern Africa at least 120 000 years ago.

The slab of sandstone at Langebaan Lagoon containing the footprints was carefully cut free and removed to the Iziko: South African Museum in Cape Town for safe keeping and further study.

An interesting Earlier Stone Age site in the Western Cape is Elandsfontein, about ten kilometres inland from the Langebaan Lagoon on the west coast. Situated in an impermanent dunefield, it has yielded significant finds of Acheulian artefacts, a human skullcap and a diverse range of faunal remains. Several thousand artefacts, including Acheulian handaxes and rare pointed flake blanks of the Middle Stone Age, have been excavated from the site. Approximately 100 000 fossil bones have been collected at Elandsfontein and are kept at the Iziko: South African Museum in Cape Town. Many of these are animal bones found in the ancient dens of hyenas that scavenged around waterholes in the vicinity. Interestingly, few bones show cut marks made by either stone or metal tools, suggesting that the animals died of natural causes rather than being the prey of early hunters.[3]

The Acheulian tradition of making bifacial tools continued for more than a million years until the beginning of the Middle Stone Age, probably about 250 000 years ago. This was when the large stone handaxes and cleavers characteristic of the Earlier Stone Age gave way to smaller tools made from the flakes of rock struck from larger cores. The core was carefully worked or retouched – mostly through further flaking – to create tools with sharpened faces or triangular-shaped flake blades. Some blades were refined through further flaking. The stone tools of the Middle Stone Age ranged between forty and a hundred millimetres in length.

THE MIDDLE STONE AGE: THE EMERGENCE OF MODERN HUMANS

With the Middle Stone Age came a change in lifestyle. Whereas the Earlier Stone Age people confined themselves largely to vegetated valleys, where plant foods were readily available, Middle Stone Age people moved out into the broader landscape, occupying sites in mountainous and lowland areas where they had greater access to a variety of edible plants and, importantly, animal foods. While plants, particularly geophytes (plants with fleshy underground structures such as bulbs, corms, rhizomes and tubers), constituted the bulk of their diet, there is enough evidence, in the form of faunal remains, to suggest that the hunting of game such as antelope and young buffalo also took place. Another feature of the changing lifeways of Middle Stone Age people was the exponential increase in the use of caves and rock shelters. An important consequence of this has been the accumulation over thousands of years of layers of occupation deposits – most of which are several metres thick – in caves and shelters throughout southern Africa. Scientific analysis of the human fossils found at two Middle Stone Age sites in South Africa – Klasies River on the Tsitsikamma coast and Border Cave, a site along the KwaZulu-Natal–Swaziland border – indicates that people living in southern Africa during this time (around 120 000 years ago) were anatomically modern humans.

The association of the Middle Stone Age with anatomically modern people raises the question of whether these first humans were modern in their thinking or not. Some archaeologists argue that they were 'modern in body, but not in mind'.[4] Archaeologists

KLASIES RIVER MAIN SITE

Klasies River is a small stream that enters the sea to the west of three discrete cavern systems on the Tsitsikamma coast between Plettenberg Bay and Cape St Francis. The caves cut deep into a one-kilometre cliff face section along the coast and are situated at heights ranging between six and eighteen metres above sea level. In the shelter of the overhanging cliff and spilling into the caves at the main archaeological site are multiple layers of deposits which have accumulated over thousands of years. Some twenty metres deep in places, these deposits are rich in fossilised debris left behind by generations of humans who frequented the caves during the Middle and Later Stone Ages.

The caves at Klasies River have yielded some of the oldest fossils of modern humans yet found. An extensive excavation of the site in 1967–8 led to the recovery of a number of human fossil fragments. These consisted of jaws, teeth and cranial pieces found in a horizon now dated to 90 000 years ago. Subsequent excavations at lower horizons revealed even older modern human specimens dating to 110 000 and 120 000 years ago. It is these finds that have enabled archaeologists to claim that anatomically modern humans were living in southern Africa at a time when Neanderthals, a related but different species that lived until about 27 000 years ago, were roaming Europe. The fossilised human remains discovered at Klasies River lend support to the theory that modern humanity first evolved in Africa.

The Klasies River archaeological sites and surrounding area have been declared a provincial heritage site. The caves are situated on private property and access to the sites is restricted to preserve the area.

Hilary and Janette Deacon, however, conclude that 'the indications are that Middle Stone Age people did think like us',[5] and that it is this capacity to think that links anatomically modern people of the Middle and Later Stone Ages with present-day hunter-gatherers (San). Based on archaeological evidence, they identified several forms of behaviour that demonstrate the existence of such a link. Among these are the formation of family foraging groups, as evidenced in the occurrence of small circular hearths associated with food waste at many Middle Stone Age sites, and the ability to form strong kinship ties. Evidence for the existence of kinship ties is indirect, but the distribution of sites in the landscape points to the ability of family groups to disband, presumably at times of food shortage, and subsequently to come together again. Further evidence of the presence of modern cognition among Middle Stone Age people is demonstrated by their capacity for symbolic communication. Archaeologists believe that throughout Africa the colours, red, white and black, conveyed symbolic meanings. Primary evidence of this ability is in the use of red ochre, found on burial stones excavated at a number of Midddle Stone Age sites in Africa. Furthermore, graphic depictions such as the patterned engravings on ochre blocks found at Blombos Cave, an archaeological site near Still Bay on the southern Cape coast, show that the first humans were capable of abstract thought. The ability to manage food resources is another example of cognitive capability. Faunal remains at Middle Stone Age sites indicate that early anatomically modern humans engaged in hunting, an activity that requires an understanding of animal behaviour and the ability to adapt hunting strategies accordingly. There is also evidence of Middle Stone Age people using fire to manage plant food resources such as geophytes, which proliferate after a burn as their growth is stimulated by nutrients released from the ash.[6]

BLOMBOS CAVE

Excavations undertaken at Blombos Cave on the southern Cape coast have led to unexpected finds of artefacts that shed new light on the debate about the origins of humankind. The artefacts include rare ochre pieces, bone points, scrapers, bifacial points and the remains of large fish, almost certainly caught for food.

Two pieces of ochre found in the Middle Stone Age layer in the cave are of particular importance, as the complexity of their design provides further insight into the development of modern human behaviour in southern Africa. The engraved surfaces of the ochre pieces were prepared by grinding the faces. One piece of ochre features a cross-hatched design with two sets of six and eight lines partly intersected by a longer line. The second face shows a row of cross-hatched lines framed and bisected by horizontal lines. The method used to prepare the surfaces and the complexity of the motifs indicate the ability to translate complex thoughts into a series of deliberate actions. It is this ability in particular that distinguishes modern human beings from earlier species in the genus *Homo* and from their ancestors, the australopithecines.

The Blombos Cave artefacts are approximately 77 000 years old. Their age and the skilful execution of their design support the theory that modern human behaviour emerged in Africa 40 000 years earlier than in Eurasia, where the most compelling evidence of cognitive capability among true humans dates to only 35 000 years ago.

There has been much debate about the origins of modern humans. Currently, two theories predominate. The first is that modern human behaviour emerged relatively recently, between 40 000 and 50 000 years ago, after which it developed rapidly. The second hypothesis holds that modern people evolved during the Middle Stone Age, commencing about 250 000 years ago. Strong support for this point of view in southern Africa is found in the technology, economy, social organisation and the use of symbolism associated with the Middle Stone Age people, all of which suggest that early humans were modern in their way of thinking.

THE LATER STONE AGE: AN AGE OF MORE PRECISE INNOVATION

The transition from the Middle Stone Age to the Later Stone Age occurred across most of southern Africa around 22 000 years ago, although some archaeologists argue that it could have begun much earlier. The main difference between the Middle and Later Stone Ages lies in the preferred method of stone tool-making. The shift is characterised by a series of technological innovations that were associated with changes in the nature of the hunter-gatherers' material culture. Toolmakers produced smaller stone tools, called microliths, as well as polished bone artefacts, engraved ostrich eggshell flasks, tortoiseshell bowls, bows and arrows, and bored stones used as weights for digging sticks. Very important for our understanding of this period is the fact that these tools were still being made by indigenous people in South Africa at the time of European contact. This means that present-day archaeologists can refer to eyewitness accounts of their manufacture and usage.

Rock paintings and engravings found throughout southern Africa are another significant feature of the Later Stone Age. Remnants of this art can still be found on the walls of caves and overhangs where Later Stone Age people once lived and are regarded as some of the region's most treasured heritage resources. Another distinguishing feature associated with the Later Stone Age is the practice of burying the dead. Evidence from the Matjes River Rock Shelter at Keurboomstrand, for example, indicates that the dead were being buried in the floors of rock shelters from about 10 000 years ago.

STONE AGE SITES IN THE WESTERN CAPE

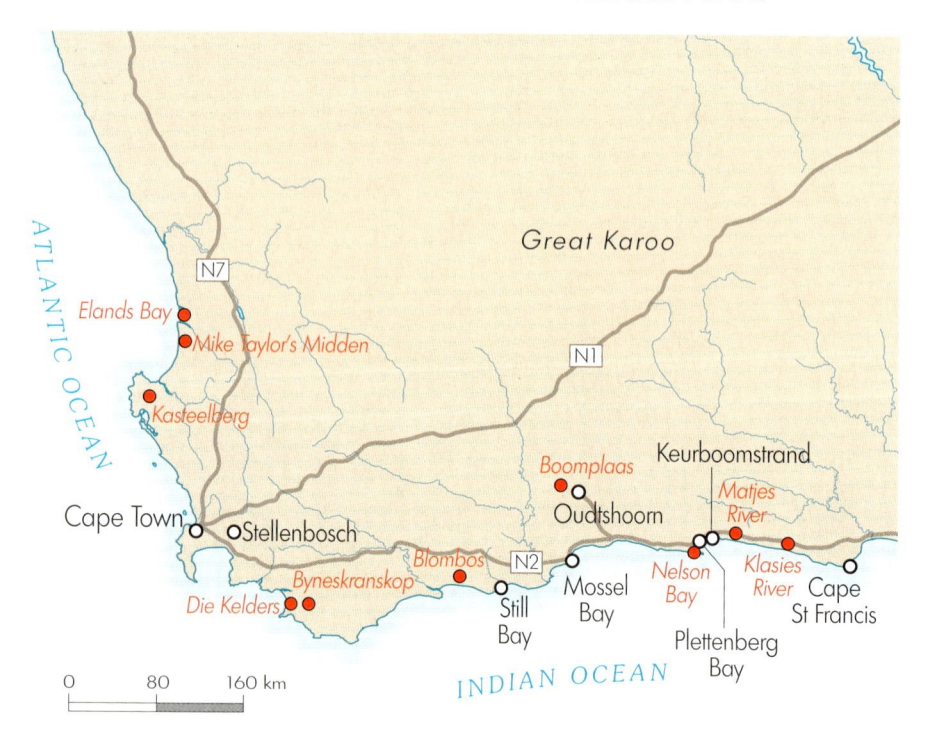

Many of the Later Stone Age sites in the Western Cape are located along the coast where water was more plentiful and food resources were in greater abundance than in the drier hinterland. People who lived at these sites gathered shellfish and caught fish in traps, which they built in intertidal zones. Important evidence of the lifestyle of coastal hunter-gathers has accumulated in shell middens, which are found all along South Africa's coastline. More than 3 500 sites have been recorded to date. Research undertaken at various Later Stone Age midden sites, including Matjes River Rock Shelter, has revealed that the people who created them were ancestral San.

THE LATER STONE AGE

Fish traps at Noorkappers Point

Archaeologists believe that the first intertidal fish traps may have been built during the Later Stone Age, between 7 000 and 3 300 years ago. The low stone barriers were erected in the intertidal zones of sheltered rocky bays and can still be seen at various locations along the Cape coastline. The stone walls were packed in such a way that when the fish were swept into the bay at high tide, they would be trapped in the enclosures when the tide receded.

One of the best preserved fish traps found anywhere along the Cape coast is at Noorkappers Point, south of the modern fishing harbour at Still Bay. Researchers have suggested that these particular traps were built by the Khoekhoen when they first arrived in the area some 2 000 years ago. The Noorkappers Point fish traps extend for about 600 metres along the shore and comprise twenty-five separate enclosures. The traps are still in use today and reasonable numbers of southern mullet (Liza richardsoni) are caught there each season. The sea harvest provides food for the local community, many of whom are dependent on fishing for survival. The manner in which the traps are used and maintained probably differs little from when they were first built by the Khoekhoe herders. The fish traps at Noorkappers Point are a provincial heritage site.

MIDDENS – RELICS OF ANCIENT TIMES

Shell middens dot the entire length of South Africa's 3 000-kilometre coastline. They are the waste dumps of early humans and as such they are a record of the exploitation of marine life by hunter-gatherers (San) and herders (Khoekhoen) during the last 12 000 years of the Later Stone Age.

From research done at Klasies River on the Tsitsikamma coast, it is clear that people utilised shellfish as a food resource in South Africa from about 120 000 years ago. However, most middens that accumulated during the Middle Stone Age were submerged when melting ice sheets caused a rise in the sea level during the Last Glacial–Interglacial cycle between 120 000 and 12 000 years ago. Some remaining Middle Stone Age middens have been found in caves along the coast, where they were protected. Later Stone Age middens occur in coastal caves as well as in sand dunes. Large open sites, or megamiddens, dating back to between 3 000 and 2 000 years ago, are found at various places along the west coast. Here people settled in larger numbers for longer periods at a time.

Shell middens can be distinguished from natural accumulations of marine shells by the presence of artefacts and the bones of animals eaten by Later Stone Age people. Many middens include the remains of birds, fish, crabs, crayfish and marine mammals such as seals, dolphins and even whales. Middens near sandy shores contain a large percentage of white mussel shells, whereas those found along rocky beaches are more varied and incorporate the shells of abalone, periwinkles, alikreukel and limpets.

Mike Taylor's Midden is situated at Mussel Point near Elands Bay. It is one of the largest megamiddens along the west coast and covers an area of at least 200 by 120 metres. Recent research at the site has led to the discovery of stone artefacts and bone remains which had been covered by enormous quantities of marine shell refuse. Based on these findings, archaeologists have suggested that in addition to functioning as a shellfish-processing location, Mike Taylor's Midden was also a settlement site.

Kasteelberg, near Paternoster, is named for the crenellated shapes of the rocks that cap its low hill. Sheltered by granite boulders, this large open-air site, situated some three kilometres inland from the sea, is significant in that it was first occupied by sheep herders (presumably Khoekhoen) between 1 800 and 1 600 years ago. The midden that accumulated here is 1.7 metres deep and contains mussel shells and bone fragments of sheep, cattle, seals, steenbok, hartebeest and mongooses. These deposits differ from the remains normally found at coastal middens, suggesting that the herders led a very different lifestyle to the San hunter-gatherers who lived along the coast.

It is likely that women collected the shellfish, probably at low tide. Large quantities of shellfish may have been dried or smoked for later consumption. Sometimes shells were used to make adornments and tools. Buttons and beads were made of alikreukel, which has a mother-of-pearl sheen, and pendants were created from cone shells. White mussel shells were often sharpened along their edges and used as scrapers.

By examining the content of these ancient refuse heaps, much can be inferred about the lifestyles of people who lived during precolonial times. From the excavated remains, archaeologists can determine their diet, what animals they hunted, what plant foods they gathered, and their settlement patterns. Middens also provide information on climatic and environmental conditions, giving us a deeper insight into the evolution of our world.

Middens are important heritage sites. Regrettably, these fascinating natural encyclopaedias are not always easily distinguishable from the sand dunes and coastal scrub in which they occur. As a result, many important middens have fallen victim to our insatiable need for development and our unchecked desire to alter the environment, often irreversibly, for our own purposes.

MATJES RIVER ROCK SHELTER

The Matjes River Rock Shelter is situated at the mouth of the Matjes River, east of Keurboomstrand. It was the first South African archaeological site to be radiocarbon dated and the results provided important evidence that the Later Stone Age began much earlier than originally estimated.

The rock shelter is of special interest because it contains one of the largest shell midden deposits yet found in a rock shelter anywhere in the world. The midden is some ten metres high, over thirty metres in length and more than fifteen metres wide. Its unusual size is the result of its close proximity to a resource-rich coastline, which formed when climates were cooler.

During the coldest time of the last ice age, about 18 000 years ago, when temperatures worldwide were five to eight degrees cooler than at present, the sea level was 130 metres lower than it is today and the southern Cape coastline extended eighty kilometres south of its present position. When the world warmed up after the glacial period, the sea level rose to eventually reach its present position about 12 000 years ago. It was at this time that the Matjes River Rock Shelter began to be used by Later Stone Age people; they continued to do so intermittently until historic times. Each generation left behind not only the ashes of the fires they had lit and the remains of the food they had eaten, but also the stone tools they had used and the ornaments they had worn. These remains provide a rich source of material for archaeological research.

The shelter was first excavated in 1929 by Professor T.F. Dreyer, then Chair of Zoology and Geology at Grey University College (later the University of the Free State). He identified five layers, each of which he associated with different Later Stone Age communities. Since then, further research at the Matjes River site has provided a wealth of information on the way of life of the communities that lived there.

A little more than a metre thick, the top layer comprised a mixture of ashes and weed bedding. Other items uncovered in this layer included the remains of several poorly preserved human skele-

The entrance to the Matjes River archaeological site at Keurboomstrand.

THE LATER STONE AGE

During the excavation of the Matjes River Rock Shelter a trench was dug between the rear wall of the cave and the midden. The walkway follows the trench and gives visitors a good view of the midden's five layers.

tons, shells and the bones of small antelope, seals and fish. Artefacts in this layer consisted of a small number of shell, ostrich eggshell and tortoiseshell beads, pendants, stone and bone tools and a small stone sinker used for fishing. Potsherds, probably deposited by Khoekhoe herders who first moved into the present-day Plettenberg Bay area about 1 300 years ago, were found in the deposit. Much of the top layer has eroded away.

Nearly ninety per cent of the second layer was made up of brown mussel shells (*Perna perna*), indicating the existence of rocky shores nearby. A little less than two metres thick, this layer contained a similar variety of bones as those found in the top layer. The artefacts recovered included polished bone tools and needles, ostrich eggshell beads and pendants, a bored stone used for weighting digging sticks and a flake that had probably been used for cleaning animal skins. Loosely buried human skeletons were also found. The second layer dates back to between 1 000 and 3 500 years ago.

The middle layer, which is a little over a metre deep, dates to between 8 000 and 4 000 years ago. White mussel shells (*Donax serra*) were found in this layer, indicating that the immediate coastline was sandy at the time. There were also well-made ivory tools, more than a hundred shell pendants and buttons, and over a thousand ostrich eggshell beads. Interestingly, the human skeletons found in this layer had been carefully buried and were covered with red ochre. One gravestone found in this layer was painted somewhere between 7 750 and 5 400 years ago, making it one of the oldest rock paintings found in South Africa.

The fourth layer yielded numerous stone tools as well as shell and ostrich eggshell ornaments dating to between 12 000 and 8 000 years ago. It also contained a high percentage of white and black mussel shells. Today, black mussels (*Choromytilus meridionalis*) are largely restricted to the cooler waters of South Africa's west coast. The presence of this species at Matjes River indicates that the sea around the southern Cape was once much cooler. Archaeologists found that although the skeletons buried in the fourth layer were generally taller than those buried in the layers above them, they were still ancestral to the San.

The base of the cave contained mainly coarse gravel and a layer of ash approximately ten centimetres thick. With an average depth of thirty centimetres, the fifth layer contained no graves, although two human skulls were excavated. A few artefacts, some shell fragments and food remains were also found in this layer.

The site was rehabilitated in the 1990s. Unstable sections were reinforced with geotextile sandbags, a novel conservation practice, and educational displays and a boardwalk were installed. The Matjes River Rock Shelter is a provincial heritage site and is open to the public. Original material excavated from the rock shelter can also been seen at the National Museum, Bloemfontein.

CHAPTER 2

The San

STONE AGE PEOPLE OF THE CAPE

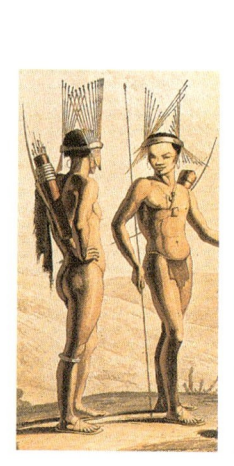

Long before the first permanent white settlement began at the Cape in 1652, hunter-gatherers lived throughout most of southern Africa. The San, people of the Later Stone Age, whose genetic origins can be traced back to the beginning of modern humanity, were the indigenous inhabitants of the subcontinent. They subsisted by hunting game with bows and arrows, foraging for roots, bulbs and corms, and gathering plants, edible leaves, wild fruits and honey. They banded together in kinship groups in territories that were widely dispersed across the landscape – from the cool and sometimes snow-covered highlands of Lesotho to the hot, dry Kalahari Desert and the temperate lowlands of the west and east coasts. The distribution of the San across the region was variable; climatic and environmental changes, and their impact on the availability of surface water and food resources, required the hunter-gatherers to adjust their group sizes from time to time.

The arrival of Iron Age Bantu-speaking immigrants in southern Africa from AD 250 impacted on the San traditional way of life. The newcomers were agro-pastoralists whose search for land to sustain their crop-growing and cattle-herding activities took them into the traditional hunting grounds of the San. Some hunter-gatherers chose to marry into farming communities, others were employed by them, while some families

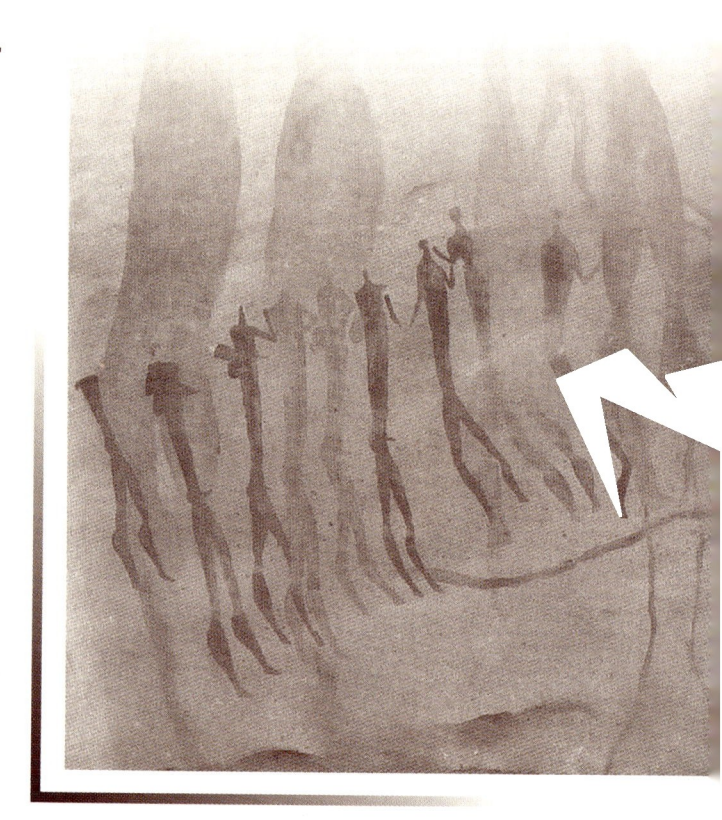

A NOTE ON NOMENCLATURE: WHAT'S IN A NAME?

There is much controversy over the words used to refer to the Stone Age people of southern Africa, who themselves had no generic term to describe their collective identity as hunter-gatherers and herders. However, when the first European travellers and settlers arrived at the Cape, the need arose for them to classify the indigenous people into generic groupings.

San

Jan van Riebeeck wrote in his diary of the indigenous hunter-gathers, referring to them as the Sonqua. The word 'Sonqua' has a number of variants, including 'Soaqua', 'Souqua', and 'Sanqua'. In some instances it was interchanged with 'Ubiqua'. It is widely accepted that these names were used by the Khoekhoen in the south-western Cape to describe the bands of cattleless people who lived from hunting and gathering. Olfert Dapper, a European writer who visited the Cape in 1668, noted in his book on African regions and their peoples that the Sonqua were an indigenous people 'who have no cattle, but live by shooting rock rabbits [and] big game'.

Another term traditionally used to describe those living as hunter-gatherers is the word 'Bushman' (*Bosjemans* or *Bossiesmans* in Dutch). Some historians attribute it to a literal translation of the word 'Sonqua', with 'son-' meaning 'bush' and 'qua' denoting 'man' in the Nama language. However, the word 'Bushman' is widely considered to be insulting and has recently fallen into disfavour.

Theophilus Hahn, the son of a Rhenish missionary and custodian of the Grey Collection in Cape Town, wrote in 1881 that the word 'Sonqua' is derived from the root 'sa-' (plural 'san') and means 'native', 'aborigine' or 'established inhabitant of the land'.[1] This equates to the Nama word 'San' (pronounced with a long *a*, 'Saan'), meaning 'foragers', which was used by the Namaqua to describe their hunter-gatherer neighbours. For this reason, the common-gender plural 'San' will be used in this book to describe the Cape's hunter-gatherers.

Khoekhoen

In his diary, Jan van Riebeeck referred to the indigenous herders of the Cape as the Quena, meaning 'people'. According to historian Dan Sleigh,[2] 'Quena' – an older form of the modern Khoina – was the name the Cape herders used when referring to themselves. The addition of the suffix '-na' to the noun stem 'Khoi' to denote the plural was, it is understood, a common feature of the south-western Cape language groups (Goringhaiqua, Gorachouqua and Cochoqua). Elsewhere, the noun stem was repeated to indicate the plural form, hence the usage of words such as 'Khoikhoi'.

The word 'Hottentot', later shortened to the disparaging 'Hotnot', was used for several centuries by European travellers and colonists to describe the Cape's indigenous herders. There are many theories about the origin of the term. The earliest recorded explanation given for the word comes from the English traveller, Edward Terry, who wrote in 1616 that the word 'Hottentot' referred to the unfamiliar click sounds in the herders' language, which, he said, 'resembled the clucking of hens, or the gobbling of turkeys.'[3] Others attribute the name to a word from a song sung by Cape herders during a traditional dance. It has also been suggested that 'Hottentot' is an altered version of an old Dutch word, loosely translated as 'stammering'. This word gave rise to the term 'Hottentotoo', which in due course was shortened to 'Hottentot'.

Olfert Dapper wrote that at the time of his visit to the Cape, the Cochoqua had a male chief named Koehque. According to well-known palaeo-anthropologist Phillip Tobias:

[T]he name Koehque is so similar to Khoe-Khoe that this may indeed indicate that the Khoi-Khoi people may originally have been known to others as the people of Koehque. By transposition from the name of the ruler to the name of the people, the name Khoe-Khoe may have become attached to the Hottentot people, by themselves and subsequently by others.[4]

Support for the idea that the Cape herders referred to themselves as the Khoe-Khoe (Khoi-Khoi) comes from John Barrow, secretary to Earl Macartney, governor of the Cape during the first British occupation. He wrote in his book, *An Account of Travels into the Interior of Southern Africa in the Years 1797 and 1798*, that

> The name even that has been given to his people is a fabrication. *Hottentot is a word that has no place nor meaning in their language; and they take to themselves the name under the idea of its being a Dutch word. When they were spread over the southern angle of Africa, each horde had its particular name; but that by which the whole nation was distinguished, and which at this moment they bear among themselves in every part of the country, is Quaiquae.*[5]

It is argued that Quaiquae and Khoe-Khoe are different spellings of the same name. After consultation with leaders of the Griqua people – descendants of the early Khoekhoen – and various academics, the collective noun 'Khoekhoen' will be used to refer to the indigenous herders of the Cape and the word 'Khoekhoe' will be used as an adjective.

Khoe-San

The term 'Khoisan' was coined in 1928 by German anthropologist Leonhard Schultze as a collective noun to describe the indigenous people of the Cape – whether hunter-gatherers or herders. He combined the word 'Khoi' ('Khoe'), the common-gender singular word for 'person' in the Nama and Koranna languages, with 'San', the Nama word used to describe hunter-gatherers.

Following modern convention, the word 'Khoe-San', instead of 'Khoisan', will be used to describe the indigenous hunter-gatherers and herders of the Cape.

There is considerable debate around the choice of terminology used to describe the Cape's indigenous hunter-gatherers and herders. Archaeologists Hilary and Janette Deacon therefore warn that

> [t]he choice of 'correct' words to describe the indigenous hunter-gatherers and herders is … fraught with problems. Like the ideas and information that history and archaeology produce, the usage will no doubt be changed in the years to come as perceptions alter and new information becomes available.[6]

chose to continue with hunting and gathering and were particularly successful in areas where the farmers could not grow crops. Gradually, over many centuries, integration took place at different levels between San and Iron Age groups. This is reflected in, for example, the adoption by some Bantu-speaking people of the click sounds typical of San languages. A further example is the existence of certain San racial characteristics, such as high cheekbone facial features and lighter skin colour, among particularly the amaXhosa.

In the south-western corner of the subcontinent the San retained greater autonomy over the land. The region, a winter rainfall area, was unsuitable for the crops grown by the Iron Age agriculturists and it thus held little attraction for them. However, approximately 2 000 years ago Khoekhoe pastoralists moved into the south-western Cape where they started competing with the San for resources such as game. Although the Khoekhoen were herders, they relied on the same water sources and spoils of the hunt to supplement their diet. This inevitably gave rise to conflict with the San, but the low population numbers of both groups and some integration, combined with the relative vastness of the land which they inhabited, meant that co-existence was possible.

It was not until the arrival of the first Europeans in the seventeenth century that the survival of the San was seriously threatened. As the land-hungry colonists consolidated their hold over the Cape, few San were left with room in which to continue their traditional way of life. They were faced with only two alternatives: to defend their territories and lifestyle or to be incorporated into the newly established colony under conditions that suited the colonists. Many chose the former, some the latter. The result was the virtual disappearance of the hunter-gatherers from South Africa. Some of those who managed to live beyond the reach of the colonists' guns remained in what became known as Namibia and Botswana. They represent the only 'ethnically pure' San left in southern Africa.

A CLOSE BOND WITH THE LAND

Contemporary ethnographic studies of San people in the Kalahari Desert in Namibia and Botswana have shown that San bands were kinship-based and consisted of a married couple with their children, a sister or brother, a cousin or close friend with their partner and children, and several grandparents or elderly relatives. The bands varied in size from twelve to twenty-five people. Each band belonged to a larger language group which had a defined territory, and within that territory each band had its own water and food resources. Others were allowed to use these resources, but only after an invitation had been extended or permission had been requested. Isaac Schapera, an anthropologist who did extensive field research among the San in the Kalahari Desert during the early part of the twentieth century, observed that:

> There are no special boundary marks between the areas occupied by different hunting bands. The limits of each area are as a rule defined by various natural landmarks, such as sand dunes, koppies, river-beds, vleis, springs, or even trees. These are well known to the people themselves and carefully observed ... In particular, however, each hunting territory is defined by the waterholes in it. These constitute the real property of the band. The encampments are always erected near them, all the game on the land around them or drinking at the water may be hunted only by members of the band, and similarly only they may gather 'veldkos' (wild vegetable foods) in the vicinity. The infringement of territorial rights in this respect is one of the main causes of dispute between neighbouring bands, and almost invariably leads to bloodshed.⁷

Peers' Cave – Evidence of precolonial life on the Cape Peninsula

Peers' Cave lies about 250 metres above sea level and overlooks Fish Hoek in Cape Town. It contains evidence of human habitation spanning the last 12 000 years and until recently was the only place on the Cape Peninsula where San rock paintings could still be seen. The site remained undisturbed until 1927 when amateur archaeologists Victor Peers and his son Bertie, encouraged by John Goodwin of the University of Cape Town, began excavations there. Their work was followed up by archaeologist Keith Jolly, in 1947, and an American researcher, Barbara Anthony, in 1963. The remains of nine people, presumably ancestral San, have been recovered from the site. Some of these date to 12 000 years ago, making them the oldest human remains found within a 100-kilometre radius of Cape Town.

In areas where there was little natural cover, San hunters used many techniques to stalk their prey. One way was to attach the branches of a bush to their bodies in order to disguise themselves. Another was to use the head, neck and feathers of a dead ostrich and to imitate its walk, a strategy that often caught grazing animals totally off guard. Paintings by Charles Bell. (Bell Heritage Trust, UCT)

The territory of each band was handed down from father to son or other relative. The occupation of a specific territory by successive generations meant that a band developed a strong bond with the landscape, which was reinforced by stories, myths and legends relating to particular features within it. American geographer Yi-Fu Tuan refers to this territorial bonding as 'topophilia', which archaeologists Hilary and Janette Deacon describe as 'the affective bond between people and the landscape in which they live that extends into a desire to stress the individuality of the group.'[8] They go on to point out that 'the power of the bond that developed between the San and their surroundings is obvious from remarks they made about the land they regarded as their own. It is also evident in their distress at losing rights to their land and being moved from one place to another in colonial times.'[9] Historian Nigel Penn, referring to the fanaticism with which the San defended their territories against settler farmers, noted that 'there was a profoundly spiritual connection between particular places and the systems of meaning that the San had constructed in order to explain their world … Thus, to lose the land was to lose, literally, everything.'[10]

CONFLICT WITH THE COLONISTS

In the late fifteenth century the growing economies of Europe required new produce and raw materials, which were to be found in territories that lay beyond the borders of continental Europe. This need inspired great voyages of discovery, initially led by Portuguese and Spanish explorers whose countries were positioned at the gateway to the New World. It was the intrepid Portuguese navigator, Bartolomeu Dias, who first landed on the shores of southern Africa when he reached present-day Mossel Bay on 3 February 1488. Although he was not able to sail on to India, his hoped-for destination, his epic voyage opened up a sea route to the Far East around Africa's southernmost point. Ten years later, on 20 May 1498, his compatriot, Vasco da Gama, landed at Calicut in India. The ships of the *Vereenigde Oost-Indische Compagnie* (VOC), known as the Dutch East India Company, soon followed in the wake of the Portuguese caravels. Trade with the East and competition between European merchants began in earnest. The VOC was a giant trading company and consisted of six loosely associated regional chambers under the supreme direction of the Lords Seventeen over whom the States General (parliament) exercised nominal control. From the beginning it concentrated on the Far East, virtually driving out Portuguese competition in the region. The VOC set up a permanent administration in the East Indies with its headquarters at Batavia on the island of Java. In order to supply its ships with fresh food and water on their journeys to and from the East and to prevent its arch-rival, the English East India Company, from doing likewise, the Company established a refreshment station at the Cape. On 6 April 1652, under the direct orders of the VOC, Jan van Riebeeck planted the Dutch flag on the shores of Table Bay and a steady process of colonisation began.

The small refreshment station established at the Cape slowly grew into a more permanent settlement. As the number of colonists increased, pressure to acquire more land for farming and grazing mounted. Within fifty years of the arrival of Jan van Riebeeck in 1652, the colony's first farmers, including Protestant Huguenots seeking refuge from religious persecution in France, began to occupy freehold grants along the Berg River. As the colonists fanned out beyond the settlement's boundaries and into the territories of the San, contact and conflict with the indigenous people of the Cape became inevitable. Those San who lived in the caves of the surrounding mountains must have watched in horror as the new arrivals began to invade their ancestral hunting grounds.

Charles Bell's 1852 painting of the landing of Jan van Riebeeck at the Cape is an uncritical rendition of the meeting between the first European settlers and the Cape's indigenous people. Painted two centuries after the event, it is a rather romanticised depiction of the meeting between people of two vastly different worlds. (National Library of South Africa)

THE SAN

Where they could, the San put up resistance against the invaders. The first major encounter took place in 1701. By then the colonists had crossed the Limietberge, the protective ring of mountains surrounding Wellington, and had spread out to Riebeeck Kasteel and the Tulbagh basin. In March of that year a group of San living in the Obiqua Mountains near Tulbagh attacked a farm owned by Gerrit Cloete and stole forty cattle. A second attack followed a month later, this time on the Company's post near Twenty-four Rivers. The Council of Policy, the Dutch colony's chief policy-making body, responded by sending a commando of forty men to recover the cattle. The men were instructed to arrest the offenders and bring them to the Castle in Cape Town for trial and punishment. Those who resisted arrest were to be shot. This was the beginning of a series of increasingly violent clashes between the settler farmers and the San. Historian J.S. Marais remarked that if the 'hunters were shot down in their tens and twenties during the first half of the eighteenth century, during the next fifty years they perished in their hundreds.'[11]

During the second half of the eighteenth century the colonists embarked on a programme of rapid expansion into the Cape hinterland. Some farmers had adopted a nomadic way of life, moving with their livestock beyond the boundary of the south-western Cape and the control of the Company in search of new farming opportunities and land for grazing. As these nomadic pastoral farmers, known as trekboers, penetrated territories to the north and east of Cape Town, clashes with the San became more frequent. In the 1770s, Robert Gordon, the commander of the Dutch garrison in the

Isolated and landless, the trekboers lived a spartan existence in search of grazing fields for their livestock. Painting by Charles Bell. (MuseumAfrica)

Cape, wrote of an encounter between Koerikei, a San leader with whom the Dutch settlers had clashed on several occasions, and a *veldwachtmeester* (a supervisor of Company cattle herders) by the name of Van der Merwe. Standing on a cliff in the Sneeuberg, out of range of the Dutch official's musket, Koerikei asked Van der Merwe what he was doing on his land. 'You have taken all the places where the eland and other game live. Why do you not stay where the sun goes down, where you first came from?' he asked. Van der Merwe replied by asking Koerikei whether he and his people did not have enough land as it was. Koerikei answered that he did not want to leave the land of his birth and that 'he would kill their herdsmen and that he would drive them away.'[12]

The trekboers ignored Koerikei's warning and continued to push into the interior. They moved north-eastward from Tulbagh across the Bokkeveld, eventually reaching the fringes of the Great Karoo. From there, some continued northwards over the Hantam and Roggeveld Mountains to the Orange River, but the majority advanced to the east, beyond the Nieuweveldberge to the Sneeuberg and into the Tarka region near present-day Cradock. They tended to skirt the Great Karoo, except after good rains when they made excursions into the normally arid region. As the trekboers expanded their areas of occupation, they encountered fierce resistance from the San. Nevertheless, the San were systematically dispossessed of their land and its resources. The invaders sought no accommodation with the hunter-gatherers. Instead, they viewed the San as vermin,[13] a nuisance factor in an otherwise unoccupied landscape which they considered to be theirs for the taking. They appropriated the water sources and, with their muskets, they all but annihilated the teeming herds of game, an important source of food for the hunter-gatherers. The problem was exacerbated by the Company's growing inability to exercise control over its subjects along the northern frontier. Weak and virtually bankrupt, the VOC's lack of resources prevented it from enforcing its authority or offering the indigenous people any form of protection, even if it had felt the need to do so. Poor communication and the vast distances in the colony compounded the problem. Until the creation of the district of Graaff-Reinet in 1786, the only official who had the power to intervene in the conflict between the San and the frontier farmers was the *landdrost* (magistrate) of Stellenbosch. But he was far removed from the centre of conflict and his field-cornets, who were responsible for law enforcement in frontier areas, were shown little respect by the 'bigotted and lawless'[14] trekboers.

GENOCIDE BECOMES AN OPTION

By 1774 the antagonism between the colonists and the San had reached alarming proportions and the Company decided to take action against the San. It appointed a commandant for the whole of the northern frontier and established a large expeditionary force – comprised of burghers (citizens), Khoekhoen and Bastaards[15] – to scour the 500-kilometre boundary between Piketberg and the Sneeuberg near present-day Graaff-Reinet in order to capture or kill as many San as possible. According to official reports, 503 San were killed and 239 captured during the first of several large-scale operations that would eventually lead to the virtual annihilation of the San in the south-western Cape. A return compiled by the Graaff-Reinet magistracy in 1836 shows that 2 504 San were killed and 669 taken prisoner along the Graaff-Reinet frontier alone during the last decade of VOC rule (1786–95). Records for the same period show that the San killed 276 colonists and stole 19 161 cattle and 84 094 sheep. However, Marais challenges these statistics and suggests that the majority of the 276 'colonists' who were killed by the San were in fact armed Khoekhoe herdsmen.[16] He also warns that official returns of stolen stock compiled from farmers' statements of their losses are 'notoriously unreliable'.[17]

Much of our information about the atrocities perpetrated against the San by the commandos is derived from reports by officials and travellers who visited the Cape in the nineteenth century. Important accounts in this regard are those of Colonel R. Collins, who toured the north-western frontier from 1808–9 on behalf of the Cape governor, and George Thompson, who travelled extensively throughout and beyond the colony between 1821 and 1824. Thompson's observations appeared in his book *Travels and Adventures in Southern Africa*, published in 1827. Both authors wrote that they had met several frontiersmen who had boasted about their raids against the San. Collins reported that he 'heard one man declare that within a period of six years the parties under his orders had either killed or taken prisoner 3,200 of these unfortunate creatures. Another has stated to me that the actions in which he had been engaged had caused the destruction of 2,700'.[18] A certain Commandant Nel told Thompson that 'within the last thirty years he had been upon thirty-two commandos against the Bushmen in which great numbers had been shot and their children carried into the Colony. On one of these expeditions not less than two hundred Bushmen were massacred.'[19] Thompson went on to describe the extent to which prejudice towards and hatred of the San had affected the commandant, who

> *in many other points a meritorious, benevolent and clear-sighted man, seemed to be perfectly unconscious that any part of his own proceedings, or those of his countrymen, in their ways with the Bushmen, could awaken my abhorrence ... The hereditary sentiments of animosity and the deep-rooted contemptuous prejudices, that had blinded Nel's judgment and seared his better feelings on this point did not, however, operate to prevent him judging properly enough in a neutral case.*[20]

Historian Nigel Penn points out that the colonists' perception of the San as 'other', from which flowed their contemptuous attitude towards the hunter-gatherers, took the war against the San into the realm of genocide:

> *To European observers, the San seemed to possess no property, political structures, religion, houses, literacy, decency or even an intelligible language. Somatically, too, they were as far removed from the European norm as any people the Dutch had ever encountered. Conscious of the achievements of their own nation, and imbued with a sense of their own superiority under God's guidance, it was hardly surprising that the colonists should imagine the San to be completely 'other' than themselves. Fear, contempt, hatred and the almost unrestrained licence to violence provided by the context of legitimate war on the furthest frontiers of European expansion, ensured that the war against the San would be marked by genocidal atrocities.*[21]

The commando raids against the San usually took place under the cover of darkness or just before dawn when San families could be found together in shelters or caves. Both women and men were killed during the raids and the children captured and distributed among the farmers as apprentices. The Company was aware of the farmers' practice of apprenticing children and made a futile attempt to control it by stipulating that apprenticeships were to be for a limited period only. But weak administrative control and the remoteness of the frontier farms prevented the Company from enforcing this rule and little attention was paid to the problem. The San children thus grew up to become slaves on the farms of their captors.

The shortage of herdsmen, labourers and domestic servants to work on the farms was an important issue for the settler farmers. However, San men were unlikely herders, and the farmers were singularly unsuccessful in getting the hunter-gatherers to herd their cattle. Furthermore, herding presented the San with numerous opportunities for escape, especially since the search for grazing took them beyond the settled areas where it was impossible for the farmers to police them. As far as the trekboers were concerned, San males had no role to play in their economy and were therefore expendable. The position of San women was different:

> [O]nce they had lost the protection of their menfolk, [women] could be incorporated into the trekboer economy either directly, as domestic drudges, or indirectly, by becoming the wives of Khoikhoi servants. Children, especially infants, were even more tractable and could be brought up to accept the life of an enslaved herder. In this case the term 'slave' is perhaps not as anachronistic as it would be elsewhere. By exterminating the parent society of a San child, the trekboers had achieved those necessary preconditions of enslavement: social death and natal alienation.[22]

THE BRITISH ARRIVE AT THE CAPE

From the time of the first British occupation of the Cape in 1795, the situation began to change for the better for the remaining San who still lived along the frontiers of the south-western Cape. When the British seized control of the Cape of Good Hope from the Dutch, they were shocked at the extent of the violence that characterised intergroup relationships along the colony's frontier. Although the San suffered severely at the hand of the farmers, the trekboers also had their grievances. They complained bitterly that neither their lives nor their properties were safe from 'the unconquerable marauders' they called 'the Bushmen'. In what could be described as a protracted guerilla war against the settlers, the hunter-gatherers mainly attacked at night; their targets were the isolated homesteads of farmers and their Khoekhoe or slave herdsmen. Farms were burnt, herders killed and hundreds of cattle and sheep stolen. However, the British government's investigations found that, on balance, the San 'were more sinned against than sinning, victims of almost continuous commando attacks by frontier farmers whose aim it was to slaughter the men and make captives of the women and children.'[23]

The theft of livestock, and the pursuit of the perpetrators by farmers, became a common and deadly occurrence as the Cape's frontiers spread outwards. Painting by Charles Bell. (MuseumAfrica)

THE SAN

TREKBOER ARCHITECTURE

Always on the move, the trekboers led simple lives. Their homes were rudimentary structures made from building materials available in the immediate environment. Using stones, mud and reeds, they constructed small, low-walled buildings or corbelled huts on their grazing lands. While these homes sheltered the trekboers from the elements, they did not always afford sufficient protection against San raiders.

Brakdak *homes*

The traditional *brakdak* (mud-roofed) house consisted of tightly-packed stone walls and a roof comprising a simple sapling framework covered with reeds and mud. The *brakdak* home seen below was built in the early eighteenth century, and is situated on the farm Niewejaarskraal near Laingsburg in the Western Cape. The structure's only window, a square opening in the wall, can be seen in the foreground. Along the back wall is a keeping-hole. A door was usually fixed to the keeping-hole to form a small cupboard in which valuables could be stored.

Nearby, a small heap of stones marks the graves of two women and five children who died in the house during an attack by a group of San.

With no access to conventional building materials, trekboers improvised with mud and stones to create brakdak *homes on their grazing lands.*

In 1843 seven members of a trekboer family died in this corbelled hut near Beaufort West after being attacked by a group of San.

Corbelled huts

In the semi-desert Karoo, where traditional building materials such as wood and thatch were not available, many trekboers and settled farmers erected corbelled huts made of stone. The technique, which requires a fair measure of skill, consists of laying the stones in successive courses that are set inwards until the sides converge at the apex, giving the building a beehive shape. The top opening is closed with a stone slab or, if it is large, with several flat broad stones.

Both circular and square corbelled huts were built by the early settlers. The windows consisted of narrow openings in the wall, covered by wooden shutters. The openings were deliberately small to prevent San attackers from entering the huts during raids. The window openings were usually built at an oblique angle to deflect the attackers' arrows.

The corbelled house in this photograph (above) was used as a 'winter house' – a place where farmers stayed after trekking down from the Nieuweveldberge (near present-day Beaufort West) in late summer so that their cattle could graze in the more fertile lowland areas. In 1843 the Harmse family was murdered in this hut by a group of San raiders. When the bodies were discovered – about a week after the attack – a commando led by Marthinus Bezuidenhout mounted a retaliatory raid against the San, who were killed to a man.

In order to put an end to the spiral of violence, George Macartney, governor of the Cape from 1796–8, attempted to achieve the impossible: to define the northern boundary of the colony and to prohibit further migration beyond it. This was the first time since 1660 that a line of limitation was drawn across the map of southern Africa. It was also the first time in the history of the colony that a governing authority attempted to understand the underlying causes of the conflict between the San and the colonists. It quickly became apparent to the British that access to food resources was a source of friction. In their thirst for land the trekboers had robbed the San of their traditional territories, thus leaving them no alternative but to starve to death or plunder the invaders' cattle. Macartney instructed two field-cornets on the north-western frontier 'to collect by subscription from the inhabitants ... a sufficient number of sheep to be offered to the Bushmen as a liberal present'.[24] The intention was to encourage the hunter-gatherers to become pastoralists. It was hoped that this would 'civilise' them, leading them to abandon their 'predatory existence'.

The success of Macartney's plan varied from place to place along the frontier. At first, many difficulties were experienced in getting the San to adopt a pastoral way of life. It was an economic activity that was contrary to their ancient traditions and, in the beginning, they tended to consume the sheep given to them instead of rearing the livestock. A further problem was posed by bands of San in remote areas who would plunder the sheep of the emerging pastoralists. A commission which toured the Lower Bokkeveld in 1805 found that stock theft by the San had ceased in 1798 – the year in which the first goats and sheep had been distributed among the remnant San bands in the area. In contrast to developments in the Lower Bokkeveld, the situation in the Roggeveld was more volatile, despite the earlier distribution of sheep among the San bands living there. The same commission found that there was a greater general lawlessness in the Roggeveld due to uncontrolled and unlimited hunting, which, it said, 'might perchance be the cause of irregularities'.[25] In this regard, Marais refers to the observations of Henry Lichtenstein, an early nineteenth-century traveller and explorer, who noted that: 'It was the old story: the average frontiersman had little respect for a frontier.'[26]

A CHANGE OF HEART IN THE NORTH-EAST

In the north-east, on the Graaff-Reinet frontier, efforts to restore the peace were met with a far greater measure of success. The enlightened administration of Andries Stockenström, the *landdrost* (magistrate) and later commissioner-general, and that of his son, who succeeded him as *landdrost* in 1828, did much to calm the situation down. They persuaded the frontier farmers to accept the reality that the existing policy of force, with its huge toll in human life and suffering, had not brought about lasting security and benefit to anyone. They encouraged the farmers to value human life and they made every effort to convince them that the San were an integral part of life in southern Africa.

The Stockenström policies required that the trekboer commandos be made subject to far greater control than they had ever been during the second half of the eighteenth century. Boer commandants could only raise a commando with special authorisation from the magistrate, and then only if the San raid had occurred on a large scale and the raiders had displayed a 'defiant attitude'. The size of a commando was restricted to 150

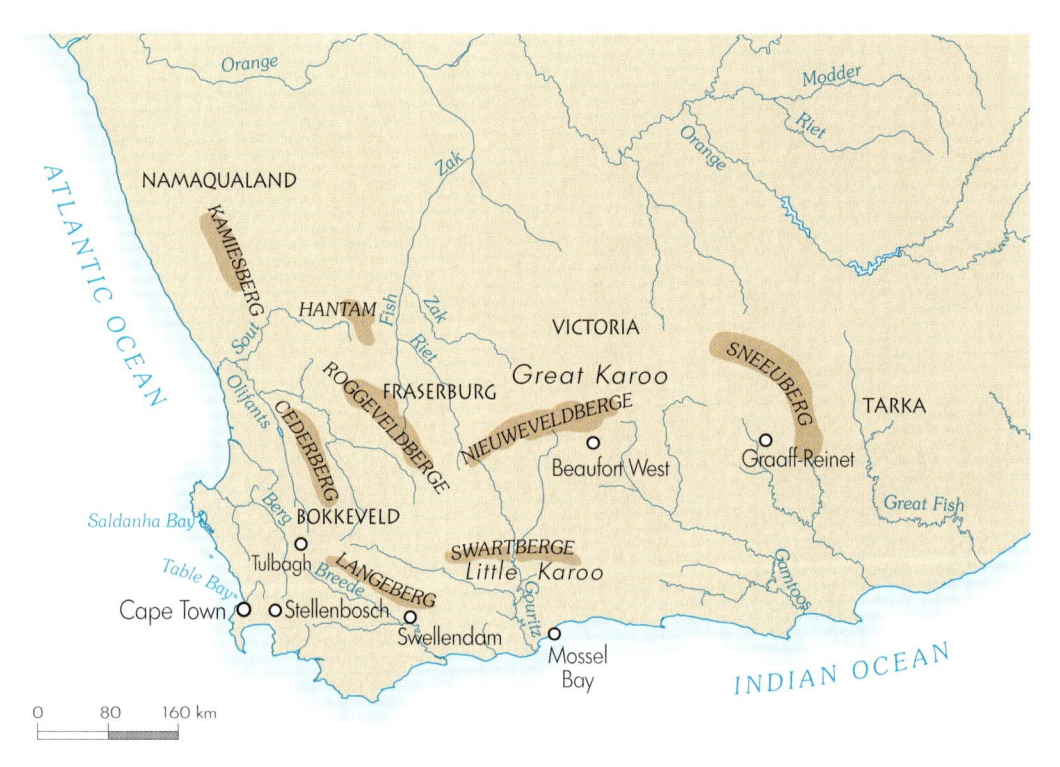

Major conflicts between the San and the trekboers took place along or near the mountains which divide the coastal lowlands from the interior highlands. These mountains, with their weather-worn crags and caves, were ideal bastions from which the San hunter-gatherers could launch their attacks in defence of their territories. Alternatively, they provided places of refuge for the San in the event of counter-attacks.

men, but the preferred *modus operandi* was to send out small parties of men under the control of a local field-cornet to recover stolen goods and, if necessary, arrest the raiders. They were instructed not to use arms unless the raiders refused to hand over the spoils. Upon their return, the commandos were required to submit a full report, including the details of any shootings. Greater attention was also paid to the treatment of captured and apprenticed San.

Farmers in the north-eastern districts began to show more concern for the welfare of the dislocated San. To counter starvation, they undertook regular hunting trips under the supervision of the magistrate in order to supply them with game. They also gave them stock in an attempt to promote pastoralism. As early as 1812, a circuit court judge reported that 'it had become a regular practice among the Boers to assist Bushman bands in their vicinity and that there were now kraals which had small flocks of goats … which had already bred'.[27] By 1820 several San groups were engaged in stockbreeding.

The Stockenströms' conciliatory policies played a major role in reducing the level of violence in the Graaff-Reinet district and creating a favourable climate for peace in the region. In recognition of this, Lord Glenelg, the British colonial secretary, appointed Andries Stockenström in 1836 as Lieutenant-Governor of the Eastern Districts. The appointment made him the highest-ranking colonist in the Cape administration in the first half of the nineteenth century. In 1839 he was awarded a baronetcy and became Sir Andries Stockenström.

THE NORTH-WESTERN FRONTIER REMAINS RECALCITRANT

Another frontier of conflict was the north-western boundary of the colony, stretching from the Roggeveld Mountains to the Orange River. Between 1820 and 1850 the British administration paid little attention to the needs of the San people in this region. At the time the mountains and plains along the north-western frontier were the combined responsibility of the magistrates of Clanwilliam, Worcester and Beaufort West, all of whom were far removed from the areas of friction. Rumours of atrocities committed against the San were rife. In 1862 Governor Philip Wodehouse asked the civil commissioner for the newly created division of Namaqualand, Louis Anthing, to launch an inquiry into events along the frontier and to attempt to restore law and order in the reserve Macartney had set aside for San occupation. Anthing's report to the Cape parliament makes for terrible reading. It chronicles the last phase of the tragic history of the Cape San and 'is the longest and best documented official account we possess of the clash between Bushman and Boer'.[28]

Anthing toured the reserve, known as Bushmanland, between February and December 1862. His information came from three sources: a trader called Nicholson, who did business in Bushmanland and whose fear of retribution made him a reluctant witness, the servants of farmers, and a considerable number of San who had survived attacks by the commandos.

According to Nicholson, it appeared that a 'wholesale system of extermination of the Bushmen people had been practised'[29] in the region in the 1850s. Virtually surrounded by their enemies, the San of Bushmanland were attacked from all sides, not only by white trekboers but also by Bastaards. The attackers came from Namaqualand, the districts of Fraserburg and Victoria, and the Bokkeveld, Hantam and Roggeveld. The San were also the target of the amaXhosa, who entered the area via present-day Carnarvon, and the Koranna, who moved down from the Orange River in the north. Nicholson told Anthing that when he first visited Bushmanland in 1858, there were numerous bands of San hunter-gatherers in the vicinity of the Hartebeest River and the lower reaches of the Zak River. At the time there were no colonists in the area. When he returned a year later, the situation had changed; he encountered few San, but found that a number of trekboers and Bastaards had settled there.

Anthing recorded accounts of two separate commando raids that took place around 1855: one commando unit consisted of trekboers, the other comprised Bastaards. The trekboers went in the direction of present-day Kenhardt, shooting virtually every San man, woman and child they came across. In all, 200 hunter-gatherers died. The Bastaard commando headed for the Karee Mountains, killing an even greater number of San by luring them to their wagons with professions of peace and promises of reward and then slaughtering them. Anthing recorded, verbatim, a poignant eyewitness account of another killing given to him by a servant of one of the trekboers:

> They [the trekboers] surrounded the place during the night, spying the Bushmen's fires. At daybreak the firing commenced and it lasted until the sun was up a little way. The commando party loaded and fired and reloaded many times before they had finished. A great many people – women and children – were killed that day. The men were absent. Only a few little children escaped and they were distributed amongst the people composing the commando. The women threw up their arms crying for mercy but no mercy was shown them. Great sin was perpetrated that day.[30]

THE CAPE SAN ARE NO MORE

The struggle between the settlers and the San in the south-western Cape continued for over a century. While it is not possible to accurately quantify the extent of the genocide, there is enough reliable evidence to indicate that the killings had a devastating effect on the hunter-gatherers' traditional way of life. Those who were not massacred during commando raids either died of new diseases introduced by the settlers or were captured and taken into forced labour. Despite a decline in the levels of violence against the San in the nineteenth century, their traditional hunter-gatherer way of life was doomed and their loss of identity and steady absorption as labourers into the lowest echelons of the colonial society became inevitable.

By 1910 the extinction of an indigenous San culture and most of the San languages in South Africa was complete. The /Xam language, which had been spoken by the largest San language group in South Africa, died out towards the end of the nineteenth century. Descendants of the /Xam continue to live in the Northern Cape, and although some of them are aware of their lineage, none of them speak /Xam or participate in traditional practices. In the Prieska area, some San descendants, referred to as the *karretjiemense* (cart people), still live a nomadic lifestyle, albeit as itinerant farm labourers. They, too, have lost access to the language, culture and traditions of their ancestors. The two largest San groups still found in South Africa are the !Xû and the Khwe, immigrants from Angola and Namibia. Approximately 3 500 !Xû speakers and 1 100 Khwe speakers currently live in tents at Schmidtsdrift near Kimberley in the Northern Cape. Many worked for the former South African Defence Force as trackers during the war in Namibia and Angola. Both groups claim an indigenous identity on the basis of their languages and cultures.

In Namibia and Botswana isolated San communities still manage to survive in semi-arid and desert areas, but their traditional way of life is under attack. A typical example of San vulnerability in current times is that of the survivors of the Gana and Gwi in the Central Kalahari Game Reserve in Botswana. Most of these people were removed from the reserve between 1997 and 2002 because the Botswana government no longer considered their tenure of their traditional homelands to be appropriate. As in the past, the hunter-gatherers were not able to put up any meaningful resistance to the predatory forces of modernisation and commercial exploitation.

The San are southern Africa's aboriginal people. Their distinct hunter-gatherer culture can be traced back over thousands of years and their genetic origins reach back over a million years, making their genetic stock the oldest of contemporary humanity. Today, their situation is infinitely tragic. They are gathered in small, disparate groups in a no man's land of societal transition. While their past has had no future, their present offers little hope, unless the self-respect taken away from them under colonialism and apartheid is restored and galvanised into sustainable development programmes. A number of non-governmental organisations have been set up to lobby for San rights and to provide training and educational opportunities. It is hoped that these initiatives will better equip the San to manage their indigenous heritage and to resist the winds of appropriation and exploitation that blow about their heads in a rapidly changing world.

THE CAPE SAN ARE NO MORE

A San woman, worn down by the harsh African sun and the poverty of her life, pauses for a moment on her long journey across the Kalahari Desert. All her worldly wealth and possessions are with her on her donkey.

SAN ROCK ART IN THE WESTERN CAPE

The history of the San people is recorded not only in their stone artefacts and the bones of their dead, but also in the rich and distinctive rock art and engravings found on the now silent walls of the caves and rock overhangs where they once lived.

The number of rock art sites in South Africa is conservatively estimated at between 35 000 and 50 000 sites. The importance of this ancient treasure is best understood when it is measured against the dearth of rock art in other parts of the world, such as Europe, where only 350 rock art sites have been recorded. The oldest known human painting done anywhere in the world is that of an eland, painted about 27 500 years ago on a wall of the Apollo 11 cave in southern Namibia. However, radiocarbon dating analyses and data from excavations show that, with a few exceptions, all the rock paintings and engravings found in the Western Cape were done within the last 7 000 years. The practice of rock art continued sporadically until the latter part of the eighteenth century.

The San made paints by grinding rock such as haematite (ochre) into a fine powder and mixing it with water, blood or plant juices to create red, maroon, yellow and orange colours. Black paint was obtained by grinding charcoal or manganese oxide and white paint was made from special clays. The red, maroon and orange colours tended to bond best with the rock, while the yellow, white and black colours faded over time. This is why some paintings appear incomplete, with only the parts painted in red and orange still visible.

This rock painting near Porterville probably reflects the visions seen during a trance experience. The elephants are surrounded by lines, which may symbolise patterns of light, called entoptics, seen in the initial stage of trance. These patterns include grids and dots as well as wavy, zigzag and crenellated lines. The elephant, like the eland, was deemed an 'animal of power', and is a common image in the rock art of the Western Cape.

People and a wide range of animals are depicted in the paintings and engravings. In the Western Cape, and particularly in the Cederberg, the most commonly painted animals are eland, elephant and smaller antelope, for example, grysbok, klipspringer and vaal rhebok. Less common are depictions of zebra, baboons and lions.

Although it is unlikely that we will ever be able to fully comprehend the significance of all rock paintings and engravings in southern Africa, research undertaken during the last two decades has focused on the religious nature of the rock art. Researchers believe that the choice of subject matter, how it is painted, where it is placed, and its posture and composition are all features related to the religious experiences of the artist.

San religion centred on the need to obtain supernatural power in order to contend with the social and economic pressures of everyday life. The San used dancing, singing and clapping to enter an altered state of consciousness in which they would receive supernatural power. Shamans (medicine people), both male and female, were the recipients of this power and they had to learn how to use and control it.

The power received during trance was used for three purposes. The first was to heal the sick. During the trance the shaman would lay hands on the sick, smearing them with nasal blood and sweat to draw out the cause of their illness. The second purpose was to make rain. The San believed that the rainmaker's spirit would leave his or her body to capture an imaginary rain animal, such as an eland, a hippopotamus or an elephant, from a waterhole or mountain top. From there the animal would be led across the veld and killed. The place where its blood or milk fell would be where the rain would come down. It was believed that large, docile animals would make soft 'female' rain, while fiercer animals would make 'male' rain or thunderstorms. The third purpose of trance was to enable the shaman's spirit to leave his or her body in order to seek out and control game, and so make the hunters' task much easier, or to locate the whereabouts of friends and relatives to ensure their safety.

Handprints are a relatively recent addition to the imagery seen on the walls of caves and shelters in the Western Cape and were probably done by Khoekhoe herders. The rhinoceros is very rarely depicted in rock paintings and engravings.

In this rock painting two groups of elongated figures appear wrapped in karosses (cloaks). One explanation is that the figures represent young men being initiated as adults. Just below the group on the left is a figure bent forward on hands and knees, probably illustrating a shaman in the process of being transformed into an animal during trance.

CHAPTER 3

The Khoekhoen

FIRST HERDERS OF THE CAPE

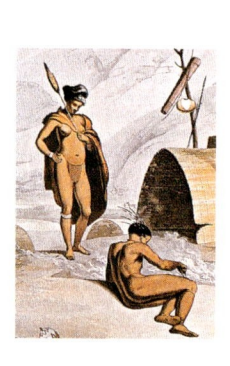

For many years the people known as the Khoekhoen were regarded as one of southern Africa's great ethnographic puzzles. In so many ways they were similar to the San, but their languages differed and they had different economies. The Khoekhoen were pastoralists and pottery-makers and the San were hunter-gatherers. Yet the ethnic boundaries that existed between them were not immutable. On occasion, usually during adverse climatic or grazing conditions resulting in the death of their livestock, the Khoekhoe herders adopted the survival strategies of the San hunter-gatherers.[1] Inevitably, this made it difficult to draw rigorous distinctions between the two groups. Adding to the confusion surrounding ethnic identity was the way early anthropologists described and classified the Cape's indigenous people.

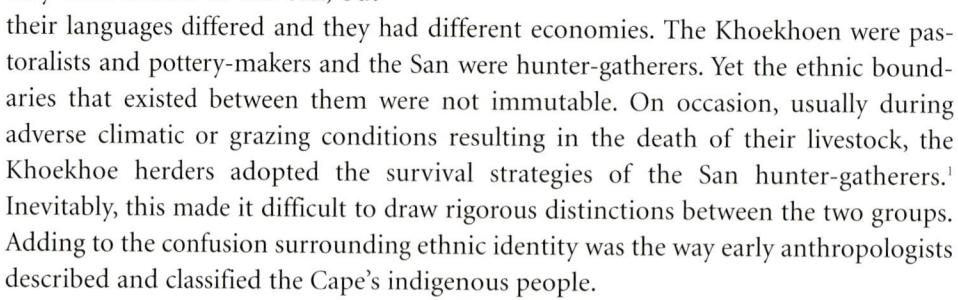

Various criteria, including physical features and anatomical size, language and economic systems, have been used to differentiate between the Khoekhoen and the San. The application of each criterion on its own, however, has its limitations. For example, the use of physical size – the Khoekhoen were generally taller than the San – as a single measure is problematic as differences in stature are more likely to be attributed to diet than to genes. Similarly, the use of language as the only criterion for differentiation between indigenous groups also has its shortcomings. This has been highlighted by the discovery that the languages of the Nharo (Naron) and the G/wi, whose descendants live in the Okavango swamps region and in the Kalahari Desert in Botswana and were originally considered to be San, have since been found to belong to a larger Khoekhoe linguistic category.

Perhaps the simplest way of viewing the Khoekhoen and the San is to accept that they came from the same stock. At some point, in the distant mists of time, they followed separate routes of development for reasons we will never know, and we should therefore consider them to be variations of an African human theme of great antiquity.[2]

THE MOVE SOUTHWARDS

A number of studies on the origins of the Khoekhoen suggest that they may have come from the middle region of the Zambezi Valley. Early twentieth-century historians George Theal and George Stow[3] postulate that the herders originated from the Great Lakes region in East Africa, from where they migrated south to the Zambezi Valley. It is thought that the Khoekhoen began their southward migration from the Zambezi region at around the time of Christ's birth, probably as a result of pressure exerted on them by neighbouring Iron Age farmers who themselves had been moving southwards from eastern Africa.

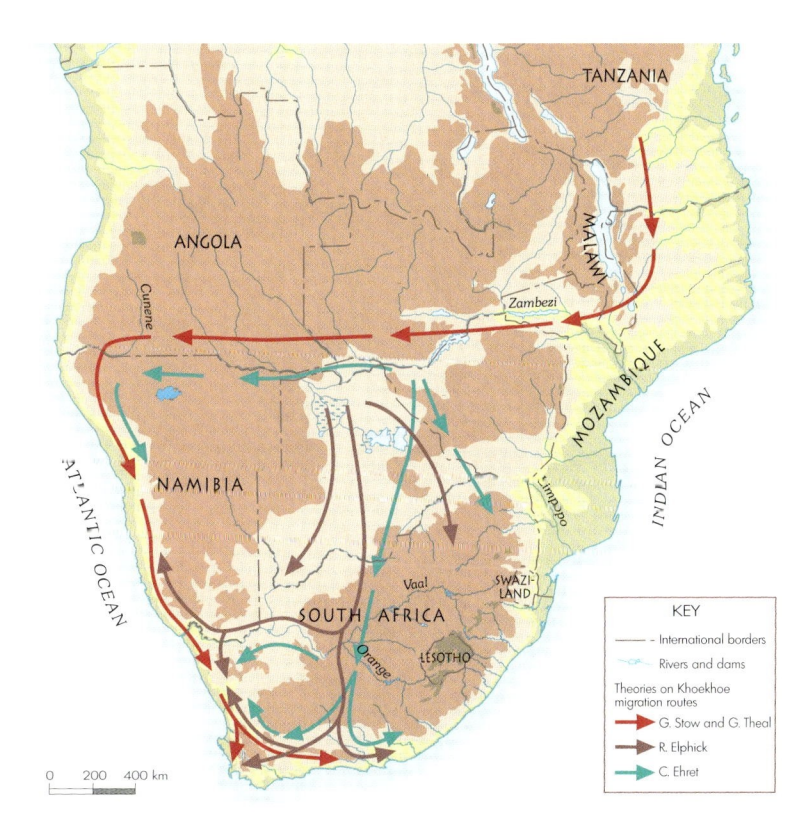

Although most historians agree that the Khoekhoen migrated into the south-western Cape from the Zambezi Valley, they differ in their views as to the routes they followed. In their thesis, Theal and Stow postulate that the Khoekhoe place of origin was somewhere in present-day Tanzania.

There are a number of possible migration routes that the Khoekhoen could have followed. Theal and Stow believe that competition between them and the Bantu-speaking agropastoralists over grazing might have contributed to their spreading south-west across the Okavango swamps and through present-day Namibia to the Atlantic Coast. From there, they moved southwards along the western Cape coast. Some Khoekhoe groups continued eastwards along the southern Cape coast as far as the Great Fish River.

Modern African historians Richard Elphick and Christopher Ehret[4] suggest that the Khoekhoen dispersed from the upper reaches of the Zambezi Valley, with one group moving south-west to the Okavango swamps and another continuing south towards the Vaal River. From the Vaal River a splinter group spread westwards to settle on the banks of the Orange River in the northern Cape. The main group, however, continued south across the highveld and the Cape's folded mountains, eventually reaching the eastern Cape coast. From there, subgroups spread along the southern Cape coast, with some settling on the Cape Peninsula and others moving up the west coast to present-day Saldanha Bay and further north to the Orange River.

A PASTORALIST WAY OF LIFE

Archaeological excavations done at Kasteelberg, Die Kelders, Byneskranskop, Boomplaas Cave and Nelson Bay Cave indicate that cattle and sheep were introduced into the western and southern Cape by the Khoekhoen about 2 000 years ago. Evidence obtained at Kasteelberg, which overlooks the fishing village of Paternoster, shows that the first stock owners in the area were sheep herders (Khoekhoen) who arrived there about 1 800 years ago. Research has revealed that cattle were introduced into the area some 500 years later.[5] Although the Khoekhoen used their cattle mainly for milk, they also used them for transport. Studies undertaken at Kasteelberg and Boomplaas Cave show that cattle were used as symbols of wealth and were acquired in far greater numbers than necessary for only milk and transport purposes. They were slaughtered on ceremonial occasions only, while sheep were used as a meat resource. At times the Khoekhoen also relied on hunting, gathering and fishing, while those living near the sea exploited marine resources such as shellfish, octopuses and seals.

Most Khoekhoe groups were nomadic, moving regularly from place to place to take advantage of seasonally available grazing and other natural resources. They made *matjieshuise* (mat-covered huts) by sticking saplings into the ground in a circle to create a dome-shaped framework, which was covered with mats woven from grasses and thin reeds. These comfortable and well-ventilated homes were portable and could be dismantled and reassembled without much difficulty.

A PASTORALIST WAY OF LIFE

BOOMPLAAS CAVE

Boomplaas Cave is located north of Oudtshoorn in the Cango Valley. It is an important archaeological site because it provides clear evidence of human occupation by both hunter-gatherers and herders. Findings at the cave show that between 80 000 and 2 000 years ago the site was intermittently occupied, probably by San hunter-gatherers. From about 1 700 years ago it was used by the Khoekhoen as a stock pen and a shelter. Circular stone-packed hearths found in association with dung in the same layer in the cave indicate that people lived in one part of the cave and domestic animals in the other. The animal bones found in this deposit include those of both domesticated sheep and small game.

Eighty per cent of the sheep bones excavated at Boomplaas Cave are those of animals less than six months old, suggesting that the cave's inhabitants culled their lambs. Because of this supply of domestic meat, the inhabitants were less dependent on game for food. Interestingly, this practice of culling corresponds with modern sheep-farming methods, whereby farmers cull up to seventy-five per cent of their lambs in a season.

To assist in the interpretation of the archaeological findings made at Boomplaas, a study of

Still today, itinerant small-stock herders in Namaqualand construct temporary cooking shelters and kitchen areas at their outposts.

Namaqua settlements in the Leliefontein area of Namaqualand was undertaken in the 1980s. The study focused on the Namaqua herders, descendants of the Khoekhoen, who used a system of outlying stock posts to manage their herds. At these stock posts they built temporary huts and prepared their meals in *kookskerms* (semi-circular cooking shelters) made with thorn branches. Informants told the researchers that during bad weather they kept the lambs and some ewes in their huts, while the rest of the flock remained outside. Archaeologists suggest that the findings of this study echo the findings of the research conducted at Boomplaas Cave. This, they conclude, indicates that Boomplaas Cave was used as a stock post by ancestral Khoekhoen. The finding is also corroborated by the cultural material found in the deposit, including pottery, ornaments and stone artefacts. The pottery is typical of the Cape coastal pottery that was widely associated with stock-keeping and which continued to be made by the Khoekhoe herders in historic times.

This traditional Namaqualand kookskerm *is made with* asbos *(Psilocaulon sp.).*

THE KHOEKHOEN

The pottery of the Khoekhoen was distinctive and included vessels with conical bases and lugs that were easy to load onto the cattle when being transported. The herders also made shaped vessels with spouts to facilitate pouring.

Traditionally, the Khoekhoen lived in village encampments comprising a hundred or so members of a clan. These village communities were organised along patrilineal lines and consisted of a group of males, descended from the same male ancestor, and their respective wives and children. Marriage was exogamous, which meant that men had to marry women from other clans. This practice ensured that clans became interlinked and grew into much larger units, or tribes, that varied in size from a few hundred individuals to several thousand. Each group recognised the authority of a headman,

This typical temporary shelter used by the Khoekhoen was made by bending a reed mat between two uprights. A second mat was used to close the rear. Painting by Samuel Daniell. (MuseumAfrica)

The Khoekhoen were nomadic and followed set grazing routes throughout the year. When it was time to move, they simply dismantled their mat-covered homes, loaded them, together with their other belongings, onto the backs of their cattle and transported them to the next destination. Engraving by Samuel Daniell. (MuseumAfrica)

A PASTORALIST WAY OF LIFE

A HOME ROOTED IN TRADITION

Matjieshuise can be seen in this rather stylised depiction of a Khoekhoe settlement at 'Cabo de Goede Hoop'. This engraving was published in 1711 in Abraham Bogaert's Historische Reizen door d'oostersche Deelen van Asia. *(MuseumAfrica)*

Traditional matjieshuise *are still being used at Khubus in the Richtersveld.*

The *matjieshuis*, a semi-permanent mat-house, was perfectly suited to the nomadic lifestyle of the Khoekhoe herders. It consisted of a taut, dome-shaped framework of saplings or thorn-tree boughs bound together with plant-fibre string. This work was done by men. Sedge mats were fastened to the structure in various patterns to regulate the temperature in the hut. Women were responsible for collecting the sedges and making the mats. This was laborious work, as the sedges had to be pierced in a number of places so that they could be sewn together.

During summer the huts were well-ventilated, with air passing through the mats and hot air escaping through the dome top. Mats at the front and back entrances were rolled up to increase ventilation and augment the light that filtered into the hut. On cold winter nights the inside walls were lined with animal skins to insulate the shelter. When it rained, the sedges absorbed moisture and expanded, making the structure waterproof. For the nomadic Khoekhoen, though, the main advantage of the *matjieshuise* was that they could be packed up and taken with them on the backs of their oxen.

The *matjieshuis* is still used by Nama-speaking descendants of the Khoekhoen, although the sedge mats have largely given way to plastic, hessian and even corrugated iron. These variant forms of the mat-covered house are found side by side with European-style houses in Namaqualand and in southern Namibia. One reason why these traditional huts have not been completely abandoned in favour of modern homes is that they are a symbolic expression of Namaqua identity. Many Namaqualand residents regard the *matjieshuis* as an important part of their cultural heritage. According to anthropologists Patricia Davison and Gerald Klinghardt, the shelter is 'one of a number of cultural objects and practices associated with domestic activities that people in all the Reserve communities of Namaqualand claim as differentiating them from outsiders.'[6] Davison and Klinghardt also assert that the symbolic value of the *matjieshuis* 'has been extended beyond Nama identity politics to that of Khoe identity in general.'[7]

Where natural building materials such as reeds and saplings are unavailable, people resort to using metal rods and pipes for the frames of their dome-shaped homes and plastic sheets, sacking and tin for the cladding.

THE KHOEKHOEN

Annual Khoekhoe transhumance routes in the south-western Cape prior to colonisation. (After Andrew Smith in M. Hall et al., Frontiers: South African Archaeology Today, *Cape Town, Oxford University Press, 1984, p. 136.)*

whose duties and responsibilities were loosely defined, except when dealing with civil and criminal matters. In such cases he was required to act as a mediator and judge. Another important responsibility of the headman was to decide on when the clan should move to new pastures and which pastures it should move to. The position of headman was hereditary and was passed in a direct line from the founding ancestor to the eldest son of each following generation.

Each Khoekhoe group had a more or less clearly defined territory in which to graze its livestock, but the low nutritional value of the indigenous vegetation (*fynbos*) and the aridity in some parts of the Cape forced the groups of pastoralists to seek new grazing pastures within their territories. The Cochoqua, for example, followed set grazing routes between Saldanha Bay and the Swartland throughout the year. The Gorachouqua and the Goringhaiqua used to graze their livestock in the early summer months on the pasturage around Table Bay. Towards the middle of summer, depending on grazing conditions, the pastoralists moved to Hout Bay, and in late summer they crossed over Constantia Nek to the southern Peninsula. In autumn they traversed the Cape Flats to spend the winter in the Boland. This practice of transhumance was misunderstood by the early European settlers who were accustomed to the conventions of land ownership and land-use exclusivity. For them, the Cape was an empty, unclaimed territory, and thus available for occupation and ownership. The itinerant Khoekhoen, who inhabited this landscape, were regarded as little more than contemptible irritants.

A MEETING OF TWO DIFFERENT WORLDS

The first contact between European seafarers and Khoekhoe herdsmen ended in tragedy. When Bartolomeu Dias reached Mossel Bay, which he named *São Bras*, his sailors went ashore to replenish their fresh-water tanks. But watching the strange ship anchored in the bay, the very first to be seen in these waters, was a group of Khoekhoe men who must surely have been very perplexed by what they saw. When the Portuguese sailors, dressed in strange clothing, came ashore, the startled herdsmen first retreated and then, as the men from the sea drew closer, ran away. But the Khoekhoen soon regained their composure and returned to the beach, only to see the sailors filling containers from a stream that flowed from a nearby fountain to the beach. According to Khoekhoe custom, all resources in an area occupied by a particular group belonged exclusively to that group, and outsiders who wanted to make use of these resources had to obtain permission from the 'owners'. The sailors, unaware of this important protocol, helped themselves to the water, which they saw as a free resource in an unoccupied land. The herders were offended by this behaviour and began pelting the Portuguese sailors with stones. Dias retaliated by drawing his crossbow, killing one man. The Khoekhoen retreated to a safe distance and the men from the sea hastily completed filling their containers and withdrew from the beach to continue their voyage of discovery.

When Vasco da Gama visited *São Bras* some ten years later in December 1497, he was more circumspect than Dias had been. Approached by a band of about ninety Khoekhoe men, he held out his hand in friendship and offered the curious, but not unfriendly, men small bells and red caps as tokens of peace. In return, the Khoekhoen gave them some of the ivory bracelets they wore on their arms. At their next meeting, a day or two later, the Khoekhoen brought some livestock and the first trade deal was struck between the Portuguese and the indigenous herders.

The Khoekhoen continued to trade with European seafarers for the next 165 years, bartering their cattle for iron, copper and brass as well as various other items of curiosity. The Khoekhoen remained suspicious of the visiting sailors' intentions, and, in turn, the seafarers were both wary and contemptuous of the diffident Cape herders. Although trade was the only point of contact between the Khoekhoen and the Europeans during the sixteenth and seventeenth centuries, reports of skirmishes between herders and mariners periodically reached European shores, fuelling perceptions that the African continent was inhabited by grotesque, monstrous cannibals.

THE DUTCH ESTABLISH A BASE AT THE CAPE

It has been argued that a favourable report submitted to the VOC by the shipwrecked sailors of the *Haerlem*, which ran aground during a storm in Table Bay in 1648, played an important role in the decision made by the Company's directors to establish a refreshment station at the Cape. The castaways lived at the Cape for nearly a year before the next ship arrived. On their return to Holland, they reported that they had been well treated by the Khoekhoen and had not been threatened by them in any way. They refuted charges of cannibalism, of which the Khoekhoen had previously been accused, and they proposed that a fort be established with 'a good commander, treating the natives

Controversial celebrations

The year 2002 saw the 400th anniversary of the establishment of the Vereenigde Oost-Indische Compagnie (VOC) and the 350th anniversary of the landing of Jan van Riebeeck at the Cape on 6 April 1652. Their combined celebration represented a dilemma for many. For some, celebrating Van Riebeeck's arrival was seen 'to perpetuate the myth that he founded the country. Other people were here first and it is about time all South Africans realised that.'[8] Some suggested that 'only clowns would celebrate their own oppression'.[9] Others saw the arrival of the Dutch at the Cape as a 'decisive moment in our country's history'[10] and therefore well worthy of celebration. In the event, both anniversaries were recognised, but celebrations were low key.

The statue of Jan van Riebeeck in Adderley Street, Cape Town.

with kindness, and gratefully paying for everything bartered from them … then nothing whatever would need to be feared, but in time they will learn the Dutch language, and through them the inhabitants of the Soldania Bay and of the interior might well be brought to trade'.[11]

Once the Dutch began to arrive in greater numbers to settle permanently at the Cape, it was inevitable that change would occur. The first to be affected by the Dutch intrusion were the Khoekhoen. Their seasonal migrations to other parts of the Peninsula and its environs, as well as their general wariness, kept Khoekhoe herders away from Table Bay. It took nearly six months after the arrival of the Dutch for the first herders to actually arrive at the fort of earthen ramparts and wooden walls that Van Riebeeck and his soldiers had built on the shores of Table Bay. Upon the arrival of the itinerant herders, Van Riebeeck and his men, who until then had to live off fish and seals and anything else they could find to eat, began trading with the Khoekhoen. Initially trade was conducted on almost equal terms: no matter how eager the Khoekhoen were for metal, they knew the value of their cattle, especially their breeding cows, and struck hard bargains.

The herders' shrewd sense of the value of their herds was based on the experience of the Khoekhoe leader, Xhoré, who was taken to London in 1613 on the instructions of Sir Thomas Smythe, founder of the English East India Company. Smythe wanted to establish a trading station at the Cape but thought it important to first gather information about the conditions there. He realised that it would take far too long for the English to learn to speak a Khoekhoe language and decided rather to bring a Khoekhoe leader to England where he could learn to speak English and provide Smythe with the information he wanted. In May 1613, *The Hector*, with captain Gabriel Towerson in command, rounded Cape Point and anchored in Table Bay. We do not know how it was that Xhoré and one of his headmen came to be on board *The Hector* on the day she set sail for England. But when the ship weighed anchor and her sails filled with the southeast wind, the two hapless men must have watched with dismay as Table Mountain slowly sank below the horizon. Although his companion died during the voyage, Xhoré eventually reached London where he was accommodated at Sir Thomas's residence. He was well treated and showered with many gifts. He learnt to speak a little English but he refused to answer any questions about his homeland. His curiosity, however, was insatiable, and he soon learnt that the English placed little value on the brass trinkets, iron hoops and bric-à-brac they offered in exchange for the Khoekhoen's cattle and sheep. This was a lesson he never forgot and one that he passed on to others when he eventually returned home. From then on, the barter price for stock was far higher in the Cape than anywhere else on the southern African coast and the Khoekhoen gained a reputation in shipping circles for driving hard bargains.[12]

With the passage of time, the Dutch settlers replaced their earth and wooden fort with a castle of stone and set about growing a garden. They established boundaries marked by thick hedges of wild almond trees designed to keep the Khoekhoen and their cattle away from the settlement. Van Riebeeck sent mounted expeditions to explore the surroundings and each returned with glowing reports of seemingly vacant land and flowing streams and rivers. It was not long before the temporary refreshment station started to expand beyond its original boundaries. Some Company employees were released from their contracts in 1657 and allowed to farm on their own along the

A section of the wild almond hedge planted by Jan van Riebeeck to separate the Khoekhoen and the Dutch settlers.

Van Riebeeck's wild almond hedge

The remnants of a wild almond hedge planted by Jan van Riebeeck in the 1660s can be seen in the Kirstenbosch National Botanical Garden in Cape Town. The purpose of the hedge was fourfold: to mark the boundaries of the VOC refreshment station; to achieve a landscape more akin to that of Europe than that of alien Africa; to erect a barrier across the traditional transhumance routes followed by the Khoekhoen; and to protect the settlers from attack. Van Riebeeck was clear about the reasons for planting the hedge:

> This belt will then be so densely overgrown that it will be impossible for cattle or sheep to be driven through and it will take the form of a protective fence, like those which some lords and squires mark off the boundaries of their territories in certain parts of Germany and in the district of Cologne. They also have circular watch- or guard-towers here and there with heavily barred entrances to protect the farmers from attacks from outside. Our already completed watchtowers and their adjacent barriers will serve a similar purpose in our case ... Within the compass of this hedge, the whole settlement and all the grain farms, forests etc. will be beautifully enclosed as in a half-moon, and everything will be well protected against raids by the Hottentots.[13]

The wild almond (Brabejum stellatifolium) is a member of the protea family and is indigenous to the Cape. It is a quick and sturdy grower, and when the trees are planted close together their branches become enmeshed to form an almost impenetrable hedge.

Liesbeek River. Known as free burghers, they were able to practise certain trades, own or rent land and hold local office. They were later joined by immigrant farmers who were also granted free burgher status by the VOC. Steadily, as more and more areas were opened up for farming, the boundaries of the small settlement were pushed across the Cape Flats and into the hinterland.

AUTSHUMATO AND THE *STRANDLOPERS*

The lack of written records on the San and the Khoekhoen in the early days of the Dutch colony probably contributed to the popular misconception that there was a separate cultural, linguistic or even racial group called the *Strandlopers* (Beachcombers). Research shows that the term '*Strandloper*' was first used by early European writers, and in particular by Jan van Riebeeck in his reports to the VOC. The last time it was used in the official records of the Cape was in March 1681.

The term '*Strandloper*' referred to a specific group of maybe seventy to a hundred people of Gorachouqua and Goringhaicona origin. The *Strandlopers* were probably outcasts who no longer led a herding lifestyle, preferring to stay in the vicinity of present-day Cape Town in order to benefit from contact with passing ships sailing between Europe and the East. The *Strandlopers* provided a number of services, which ranged from carrying fresh water and locally available food and other supplies to the sailors' boats to acting as intermediaries for sailors wanting to trade with the Khoekhoen. They also served as a kind of 'postmaster' for ships that called at Table Bay and supplied ships' captains with intelligence on rival fleets and on conditions in the immediate hinterland.

The best-known leader of these coastal scroungers was Autshumato. He was jokingly called King Harry by an English captain who took him to Bantam in the East Indies in 1631. Autshumato learned to speak English during the long voyage to the East and, after his return to the Cape two years later, fulfilled a useful role as interpreter and negotiator for Europeans wishing to trade with the Khoekhoen. Twenty years after his journey to Bantam, Autshumato acted as a broker for Van Riebeeck and negotiated on behalf of the Dutch with various Khoekhoe groups to obtain cattle and sheep.

In October 1653 Autshumato and his followers made off with the Company's cattle after murdering the Dutch herder, David Jansz. Autshumato was arrested and would almost certainly have been put to death had it not been for the intervention of Krotoa, Van Riebeeck's enigmatic domestic servant and Autshumato's niece. A perceptive negotiator, Krotoa pleaded for clemency on her uncle's behalf and, heeding her call, Van Riebeeck banned the wily chief to Robben Island. He was released two years later and reinstated to his position as interpreter at the fort.

Despite his fall from grace, Autshumato was still able to manipulate the system to his own advantage. He began to build up cattle stocks and eventually became a relatively wealthy man. In July 1658 his fortunes were set to change once again. After a number of slaves had escaped from the fort, Van Riebeeck took Autshumato hostage, hoping that it would encourage the *Strandlopers* to capture the slaves and thus secure the release of their chief. He was first imprisoned at the fort before being transferred to Robben Island.

In 1659 the incorrigible Autshumato escaped from the prison island in a leaky boat and landed somewhere near Bloubergstrand. Instead of being rearrested, he was reappointed to his old position at the fort. But his time had passed, and he never regained his wealth and position of influence.

Other Khoekhoe interpreters had taken over his role as interpreter and negotiator and they had an advantage over him: they had learnt to speak Dutch, whereas Autshumato could only speak English. Autshumato died in 1663, a year after Van Riebeeck left the Cape.

CONFLICT ERUPTS

The encroachment on the Khoekhoen's pasture lands by the Dutch set the scene for open conflict between the Company and the Cape herders. The Dutch settlers regarded land as a commodity, which had monetary value and could be privately owned, exchanged or sold. For the Khoekhoen, land and the grazing it yielded were common property resources whose usage by the community was subject to certain customary practices. The land itself was not available for personal acquisition or sale. Disputes over the bartering of cattle exacerbated the tension. The demand for meat from passing fleets steadily increased and Company employees had to find more trading partners among the Khoekhoen in order to obtain enough stock to provision the ships. This was not a simple matter. There was a fundamental difference in attitude between the Khoekhoen and the Dutch towards the ownership of cattle. The Khoekhoen regarded their cattle as symbols of wealth and were reluctant to use them as items of trade. For the Dutch, however, livestock, like land, was a commodity and therefore had financial and exchange value. The Dutch misunderstood the Khoekhoe herders' reluctance to part with their cattle and they increasingly grew wary of the herders' motives.

These mutual misunderstandings led to the first Khoekhoen–Dutch skirmish, in 1659. Angered by the cultivation of prize grazing land by the colonists, a band of Khoekhoe men 'confiscated' seven of the Company's draught oxen in the hope that the farmers would discontinue their agricultural activities. In response, the newly established burgher militia was sent out to recover the stolen animals. Fighting broke out, resulting in the arrest of the Khoekhoe chief, Autshumato, or, as the Dutch called him, Harry (also Herrie) the *Strandloper*.

Tension between the Khoekhoen and the Dutch settlers continued to simmer. In an attempt to contain the situation, the Dutch concluded two treaties with the Goringhaiqua and the Gorachouqua in 1672. In terms of the agreements, the Goringhaiqua and the Gorachouqua agreed to surrender large tracts of land stretching from Table Bay in the south to Saldanha Bay in the north and across to the Hottentots Holland Mountains in the east. Possibly unwittingly, they also agreed to render an annual tribute in livestock and to allow the Dutch authorities to involve themselves in certain aspects of their domestic affairs. The two Khoekhoe groups received very little in

KROTOA

We do not know much about Krotoa's early life other than that she was the daughter of a Cochoqua chief and became a servant in the Van Riebeeck household when she was a teenager. Baptised as 'Eva' in the Dutch Reformed Church, Krotoa adapted well to European customs and soon became an important mediator between the local Khoekhoen and the Dutch. She had remarkable linguistic skills and apparently was fluent in Dutch and could speak both English and Portuguese. Van Riebeeck considered Krotoa to be an adept negotiator, although he never totally trusted her. She partially misled him during his negotiations with the Cochoqua at the time of the 1659 Khoekhoen–Dutch war, and this contributed to a growing estrangement between her and the Company.

While in the employ of Van Riebeeck, Krotoa attracted the eye of Pieter van Meerhoff, a settler at the Cape from the Dutch quarter of Copenhagen. When Van Meerhoff was transferred to Robben Island as the Company's postholder in 1664, the couple decided to get married and a 'a little wedding feast' was given in their honour at the fort. From all accounts, however, it was not a happy union, and Eva, torn between the two worlds she endeavoured to straddle, took to finding solace in the white man's bottle. Van Meerhoff was eventually killed in Madagascar while on a slaving expedition. Krotoa, rejected by both her people and the Company, died of alcohol abuse in 1674.

return. By 1700 several proclamations had been passed which regulated virtually every aspect of herder-settler relations.

Steadily, a legally based social hierarchy began to evolve in the Cape. Company servants were in the most elevated position, followed by free burghers, free blacks (ex-slaves and their descendants and freed exiles who had been banished to the Cape by the VOC), slaves and the Khoekhoen.

STATUS OF THE KHOEKHOEN

Although Van Riebeeck initially wanted to enslave the Khoekhoen, the directors of the VOC were not prepared to sanction such a move. The Company's negative experiences with the enslavement of local people in Batavia caused it to be more circumspect in its dealings with the indigenous population of the Cape. Technically, the Khoekhoen were viewed as free and independent people. Practically, however, the ability of the Khoekhoen to maintain their independence was eroded by the steady loss of their economic means to do so. Deprived of access to the land and permanently cut off from their traditional grazing routes they had no alternative but to barter away their dwindling herds. The herders' eventual loss of their livestock and their inability to stem the tide of settler expansion marked the end of their traditional way of life, and the beginning of their incorporation into the wider Cape society.

In many ways the Khoekhoen had the worst of two worlds. Although they were technically free and independent, they could not own land and did not enjoy the same rights as the settlers. On the other hand, since they were free and independent, they could not expect protection and maintenance from their masters, as the slaves could. They were subjected to vigorous control by colonial officials, many of whom saw little reason to exercise the same restraint in their dealings with the Khoekhoen as they did in their treatment of the slaves. Slaves were purchased and owned and therefore represented capital from which a return could be expected. Disease, too, took its toll on the indigenous population. An outbreak of smallpox in the Cape in 1713 had a devastating effect on the Khoekhoen (and slaves), who had no immunity against the disease.

Despite serious disruptions to their lives during the eighteenth and nineteenth centuries, some Khoekhoen, especially those in remote areas such as Namaqualand, still managed to maintain a measure of independence. Painting by Charles Bell. (MuseumAfrica)

Despite these adversities, the Khoekhoen went to considerable lengths to avoid being enslaved, a condition which they considered to be utterly repugnant. They refused to take on long-term work contracts or commitments for fear that these should tie them down, thereby reducing their status to that of slaves. Instead, they only worked

SMALLPOX AND KHOEKHOE LABOUR

A severe smallpox epidemic broke out in Cape Town in 1713, decimating the local Khoekhoe population. Many fled into the hinterland to escape the deadly grip of the strange disease brought by the people from Europe. François Valentijn, an itinerant preacher, painted a vivid picture of its devastation:

> As to the Hottentots, they died as if by hundreds, so that they lay everywhere along the roads as if massacred as they fled inland with kraals, huts and cattle, all cursing the Dutch, who they said had bewitched them, hoping to be free in the hinterland from this evil sickness. Afterwards as a result (as I found in 1714) very few Hottentots were to be seen here compared with previously, this causing very great inconvenience to the burghers and other inhabitants who now lacked their services, both for cleaning and scouring almost everything in the house at low pay, but especially in the cutting of corn and grapes.[15]

The epidemic highlighted the colonists' vulnerability in respect of the supply of labour. To address this, legislative and other attempts were made to coerce Khoekhoe labourers to work on the colonists' farms, particularly during the harvesting season, and to enforce labour contracts more stringently. Khoekhoe women were brought into the households to serve as domestic servants. In due course, their offspring from slave fathers were bonded to the farmers until the age of twenty-five. Many remained on the farms for they knew no other life, and this provided farmers with greater labour security.

for as long as it took to obtain enough money to meet their immediate needs. Over the entire 180-year slavery and apprenticeship period, they managed to hold on to their distinct status as free and, more or less, independent people. An English traveller in the Cape in the early part of the eighteenth century wrote that the Khoekhoen 'have a great love for liberty, and an utter Aversion to slavery. Neither will they hire themselves in your service longer than from Morning to Night, for they will be paid and sleep Freemen, and not Hirelings.'[14]

By the late eighteenth century most Khoekhoen had little alternative but to look for work on farms or enter the labour force in Cape Town or in the small towns that sprang up in the outlying districts. Some chose to live by their wits in a nomadic and footloose way. Most inhabited a twilight world in which they had no legal rights and no substantive way of making a living. Landless, classless and mostly jobless, they led a precarious existence. As a result of this hopeless situation, a number of mission stations were established to provide places of refuge for some of the displaced Khoekhoen.

AN AMBIVALENT RELATIONSHIP

Ambivalence characterised relations between the colonists and the Khoekhoen right from the beginning. Van Riebeeck's hedge of wild almond trees was a forlorn attempt to create a physical barrier between the colonists and the Khoekhoe herders. The hedge did not keep the Khoekhoen out, nor did it keep the colonists in. In time, it was superseded by an incorporeal racial and class barrier that ensured that the once independent Khoekhoen were relegated to the position of menials. Denied the means to maintain their freedom and independence, they became indigent wanderers on colonial property. Subservience became the only route to their survival. Some became servants, others hawkers, fishermen or tradesmen. Some joined the militia and fought alongside the colonists. Some attempted to maintain their autonomy and trekked into the hinterland. Inevitably, the Khoekhoen lost their identity as a distinct cultural group. Assimilation meant that cultural practices associated with religion, marriage and social life changed. Most indigenous languages disappeared as the Khoekhoen adopted the Dutch language. Together with the slaves, they played an important role in its transformation to present-day Afrikaans.

Another form of ambivalence in the relationship between the colonists and the Khoekhoen arose between men and women at an intimate and personal level. Since the early days of the colony, non-marital unions of varying durations took place between Europeans and the Khoekhoen. For many years there was a heavy preponderance of males in the colonial service, and it was thus not unheard of for a European man to enter into a permanent relationship with a Khoekhoe woman, taking her as his 'wife', or, alternatively, to consort with a local woman on a short-term basis. Often both parties would be treated as outcasts of their respective societies.

Irregular or short-term unions between burghers and Khoekhoe women became entrenched in the social fabric of Cape society, especially after white stock farmers began the practice of adopting Khoekhoe women as their 'wives' when taking their cattle to new grazing lands on the other side of the Boland mountains. It was not unusual for stock farmers, married or unmarried, to associate with

As colonialism took root in the Cape many Khoekhoen became displaced. Some lived in servitude, whereas others eked out a living on the fringes of society. Painting by Thomas Baines. (MuseumAfrica)

This pen and ink drawing depicts the ambivalent relationship that developed between the colonists and the Khoekhoe herders. Colonial buildings are juxtaposed with a Khoekhoe settlement. A Khoekhoe woman, dressed in traditional clothes, seemingly challenges the viewer to consider the dilemma. (National Library of South Africa)

Khoekhoe women during the long, lonely nights spent in the hinterland. Even though society generally turned a blind eye to these liaisons, a burgher who took a Khoekhoe woman to be his wife invariably lost caste among his own people. Because of racial prejudice, the children of these unions could not hope to be included in burgher society. They were called Bastaards and their status was no different to that of the Khoekhoen. By the early nineteenth century they had become sufficiently numerous to form a separate ethnic grouping known as the Basters. In 1868, as a result of racial pressure, many of the Basters migrated to Namibia, where they maintain a separate identity to this day. Others found a home with the Griqua, an established population group within the complex South African human matrix.

Added to this mix was the high level of miscegenation that occurred between male slaves and Khoekhoe women. As late as 1708 the ratio of adult male slaves to female slaves was six to one. Although this ratio was to become better balanced over time, interracial sexual contact was inevitable, resulting in a steady increase in progeny of mixed parentage.

As the European settlement at the Cape expanded, land around the Peninsula became scarce and stock farmers were compelled to look for new grazing fields beyond the Boland mountains. (Old Mutual Collection)

THE ENGLISH OCCUPY THE CAPE

Between 1795 and 1814 the Cape changed hands three times: from the Dutch East India Company to British rule in 1795, from British to Batavian rule in 1803, and back to British rule in 1806. The arrival of the English marked the beginning of a process of statutory changes, which ultimately resulted in the recognition of the Khoekhoen as politically free and equal citizens. The first step took place after slave trading was abolished in 1807 in all of Britain's colonies. With no new slaves arriving in the Cape, greater importance was placed on the need for Khoekhoe labour. As a result, the labour status of the Khoekhoen was recognised in law for the first time. The next step aimed at regulating labour laws governing the Khoekhoen took place in 1809 when Governor Caledon, the first governor under the second British occupation, proclaimed that the 'Hottentot in the same manner as all inhabitants'[16] must have a fixed place of abode and that all the Khoekhoen living within the colony would be subject to the colonial courts of law. The Khoekhoen had to register at the local magistrate's office and were not allowed to move from their local area without a pass. All labour contracts for periods in excess of one month had to be recorded at the office of the fiscal (a Company official who served as a public prosecutor and had authority over all the slaves), a magistrate or a field-cornet. Upon leaving their place of service, all Khoekhoe labourers had to report to the field-cornet of the district, who issued them with passes and gave them a limited period, the duration of which was solely at the discretion of the field-cornet, to find a new master. Although the law, known as the Caledon Code, had the effect of coercing all Khoekhoen into the service of the colonists, it also contained certain provisions aimed at protecting servants against the abuse of power by their employers. In terms of the law, then, the Khoekhoen began to be seen as part of the Cape colonial community and not simply as 'idle, stupid, thieving appendages'.[17]

The Caledon Code was followed by two other laws. The first, passed by Governor John Cradock in 1812, made provision for the apprenticeship of servants, allowing employers to apprentice their servants' children over the age of eight for a period of ten years without remuneration. If a farmer refused or was found unfit to carry out his responsibility towards his apprentices, the *landdrost* had the authority to bind the children in question as apprentices to another more 'suitable' employer in the same district.[18] A proclamation issued in 1819 and amended in 1823 decreed that any Khoekhoe child of a mother who had died or who was unable to care for her child would be 'apprenticed to Christian inhabitants of known and acknowledged humane disposition and good character until age 18'.[19]

Although these laws contributed to a decrease in labour brutality on the farms, they did not go far enough in guaranteeing equal rights for the Khoekhoen. Missionaries, led by Dr John Philip of the London Missionary Society, argued that the Caledon Code and the supporting legislation were discriminatory and condemned the Khoekhoen to a perpetual state of servitude. Philip wrote that:

> *for no sooner is the period of their contract for serving one inhabitant expired, but it becomes necessary for them to enter into service again; and the only option left to the Hottentot, is, whether he will engage himself to the same master, or to another. Their condition, therefore, is, in this respect, more deplorable even than that of the slaves, for the latter have generally a hope, however faint, that they may possibly one day obtain their freedom.*[20]

In addition to their attack on the labour laws, the missionaries also lobbied for improvements in the administration of justice. In January 1828, legal reforms, including the appointment of resident magistrates and clerks of the peace and the introduction of a jury system, came into effect, which contributed to the achievement of equal status for all 'free' persons (non-slaves) at the Cape. Yet the Khoekhoen still lacked certain fundamental rights such as the right to private ownership of land. This and other shortcomings were addressed with the promulgation of Ordinance 50 in July 1928. It dealt with the issue of fundamental rights, stating in its second clause that 'no Hottentot or other free person of colour, lawfully residing in this Colony, shall be subject to any … hindrance, molestation, fine, imprisonment, or punishment of any kind whatsoever, under the pretence that such person has been guilty of vagrancy or any other offence, unless after trial in due course of law'.

The ordinance granted the Khoekhoen the right to own land, freed them from carrying passes, and released them from any special obligations other than those that were common to all citizens. It stipulated that oral service contracts were to be binding for one month only, and that all other service contracts, which were limited to one year, had to be registered with a competent authority. Under the ordinance, the practice of apprenticeship was reformed. Children could only be apprenticed with their parents' consent, and the children of servants whose contracts had expired could be released from their apprenticeships. The new ordinance exploded the notion that the Khoekhoen were somehow a sovereign and independent people, outside the ambit of the colonial authority's laws and concerns. It also ended the colonists' belief that the Khoekhoen were not entitled to any rights and that they were merely landless sojourners to be tolerated solely for the labour they provided.

Ordinance 50 went a long way to redress some of the major indictments of the colonial judicial system as far as the Khoekhoen were concerned, and it heralded a new era in the political status of free persons of colour in the Cape. From the promulgation of Ordinance 50 to the passing of the Statute of Westminster and the creation of the Union of South Africa in 1910, legislation in the Cape was officially

Dr John Philip (1777–1851)

Dr John Philip of the London Missionary Society was forty-two years old when he came to the Cape in 1819. The following year he was appointed superintendent and given the responsibility to develop and expand the Society's missions in southern Africa.

He was largely self-taught and very capable, but somewhat self-opinionated, autocratic, unscrupulous and arrogant. He attacked the colony's discriminatory labour policies towards the Khoekhoen in his two-volume work Researches in South Africa *(1828) and campaigned for equality between Khoekhoe labourers and settlers. To some considerable extent, it was due to his lobbying that the Cape authorities promulgated Ordinance 50 of 1828, granting all 'Hottentots and other free persons of colour' residing in the Cape the same rights as the settlers.*

Philip was also strongly opposed to slavery and advocated the abolition of slavery and the extension of full and equal citizenship rights to all emancipated slaves. His strong views on Khoekhoe rights and the emancipation of slaves made him unpopular with many of the Cape's settlers who considered him a troublesome missionary.

'colour-blind'. However, unfettered equality was not to be. Historian J.S. Marais reminds us that '[i]t was impossible, by a single piece of legislation, to destroy the slave owning mentality, or to make the Hottentots and the slaves worthy of the freedom which had been suddenly thrust upon them. Time alone could not cure the evils which time had wrought.'[21]

Sundry attempts were made by the Cape Legislative Council to turn the political clock back to pre-1828 days, particularly as a result of the effect Ordinance 50 had on the vexing problems of vagrancy, stock thieving and the shortage of labour throughout the colony. But the British Colonial Office vetoed these attempts, creating a sense of despondency, particularly among the frontier farmers, who, after the statutory emancipation of their slaves, decided to trek into the interior to escape British rule and establish their own republics and their own laws.

Statutorily free but without a vote, this then was the position of the Khoekhoen in 1834. For nearly two centuries they had been in intimate contact with colonists and with European culture. Through a steady process of acculturation, they had lost their own languages, religion and cultural heritage. Along the remote fringes of the colony, where contact between the Khoekhoen and the colonists was minimal, some Khoekhoe languages and cultural practices remained intact. While the political rights of the remaining Cape San, the Khoekhoen, the Basters, the emancipated slaves and the progeny of mixed unions, who collectively became known as the 'Cape coloureds', were entrenched in law by 1834, the impenetrable barrier of racial prejudice remained, restricting people of colour to positions of continued social inferiority. This barrier was further reinforced by economic disparities created by unequal access to and a loss of usufruct of the land and its resources.

In this painting Charles Bell depicts a travelling family. The unrestricted movement of Khoekhoe people between town and country only became possible after the promulgation of Ordinance 50 in 1828. (Bell Heritage Trust, UCT)

MISSION STATIONS – PLACES OF REFUGE FOR THE LANDLESS

The increase in missionary activity in the Cape followed on the heels of an evangelical revival that had swept across Europe during the latter part of the eighteenth century. Many of the missionaries who came to the Cape were artisans from the working and middle classes of Europe. What they lacked in formal theological education they more than made up for in technical knowledge and expertise – abilities that were put to good use in establishing their mission stations in remote and rugged places. In addition, they were well-equipped to provide skills and industrial training and promote agriculture among their followers. By 1911, thirty missionary societies and 1 650 full-time missionaries were active in southern Africa.

The mission stations in the Cape became important places of refuge for the indigenous Khoekhoen. Dispossessed of their ancestral grazing lands and other natural resources by the Dutch and unable to compete for land with the technologically advanced English settlers, the former herders moved to the mission stations – the only places where relatively large groups of Khoekhoen still lived in the south-western Cape during the nineteenth century.

Genadendal

The first mission station in the Cape was opened by the Moravian Missionary Society at Baviaanskloof near Caledon in 1737. However, pressure from neighbouring farmers forced the Society to abandon the mission station in 1743. It was reopened in 1792. Its growth as a place of settlement and as a refuge for displaced Khoekhoen grew rapidly thereafter and it was renamed Genadendal (Vale of Grace).

By 1802, 1 234 people were living at Genadendal and the settlement was the second largest in the colony at the time. It continued to thrive and by the mid-1800s, 3 450 people had moved there, making it comparable in size to Graaff-Reinet.

In addition to its ecclesiastical work, the Moravian Missionary Society sought to promote self-sufficiency by creating local industries, improving agricultural practices and providing a basic education, all within a strict religious framework. Genadendal soon became a model settlement and was the object of study for a number of other missionary movements. It was an important educational centre: the first teachers' training college in southern Africa was established there in 1838 and a number of industrial enterprises, such as a cutlery factory, a printing works and a mill, were developed.

The spatial organisation of the Moravian mission stations followed a particular land-use pattern, known as the Hernnhut model. In terms of this model, land adjacent to the mission buildings was made available for occupation by church members. Each family was granted a plot on which to build a house (according to standards laid down by the mission) and establish a domestic garden for the cultivation of fruit and vegetables. In addition, communal land was established for large-scale agriculture and grazing.

The buildings surrounding Genadendal's Church Square constitute one of the most important concentrations of nineteenth-century architecture in the Cape and have been proclaimed provincial heritage sites.

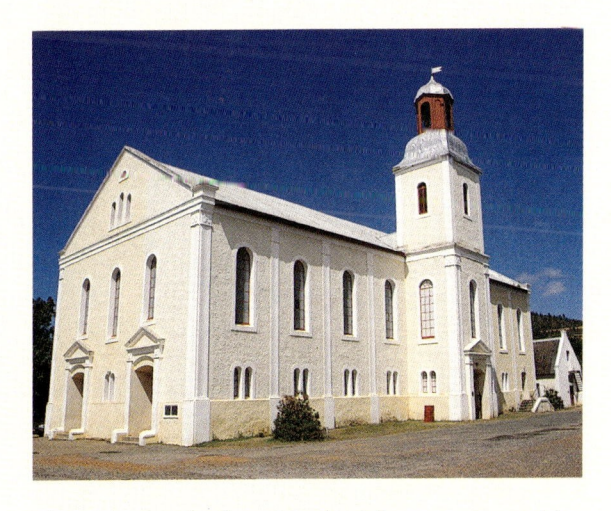

This Moravian church at Genadendal was consecrated in 1891. The double-storey building has galleries inside with separate seating for men and women.

In 1995, in recognition of the important role that the Genadendal mission station had played as a place of refuge and as a symbol of hope, former South African president Nelson Mandela renamed his official residence in Cape Town Genadendal.

Mamre

In view of the success achieved at Genadendal, the Earl of Caledon, the first governor in the Cape after the second British occupation in 1806, asked the Moravian Missionary Society to establish a second mission in the buildings of the old VOC military post at Groene Kloof on the west coast just north of Cape Town.

The Moravians readily accepted this offer and the missionaries Küster, Kohrhammer and Schmitt established a mission station there in 1808. The church was completed in 1818, making it the oldest Moravian church in South Africa and the fifth oldest church building in the country. By 1845 the population of Groenkloof (as it was now written) had grown to 1 347 inhabitants. In 1853 Groenkloof was renamed Mamre and it formed the nucleus around which a 'coloured group area' was proclaimed in terms of the Group Areas Act of 1950. It was later proclaimed a decentralised industrial area and the dormitory town of Atlantis was established nearby. The church and the historical buildings of Mamre are provincial heritage sites.

Originally used as barracks by VOC soldiers, the Long House at Mamre today provides administrative and residential accommodation for the mission.

Elim

Elim was established on an existing farm, Vogelstruyskraal, situated in the coastal strandveld between present-day Bredasdorp and Gansbaai. It was purchased by the Moravian Missionary Society in 1824 and was laid out according to the Hernnhut model. As the early missionaries had security of tenure, access to virtually virgin territory, and the experience gained at both Genadendal and Mamre to inform their planning and development decisions, Elim represents one of the best examples of an early nineteenth-century Moravian mission station. Its historical buildings have been proclaimed provincial heritage sites.

The dominant vernacular architecture of Elim is evident in this row of cottages built in a simple but pleasing style.

Wupperthal

Founded by Johann Leipoldt and Theobald von Wurmb in 1830, Wupperthal was the first Rhenish mission station in South Africa. It was established on the farm Rietmond in a very pretty but isolated valley in the foothills of the Cederberg some seventy kilometres from present-day Clanwilliam.

Due to the remote location of the mission station, self-sufficiency was imperative. Leipoldt, who had been a shoemaker in Germany, set about establishing a shoe factory, for which Wupperthal is still famous. He expanded the enterprise to include hat-making, glove-making, carpentry and tanning. Between 1830 and 1850 Wupperthal grew into a flourishing and financially independent settlement.

PLACES OF REFUGE FOR THE LANDLESS

The mission church at Wupperthal. In the 1840s transepts were added to the north and south faces, giving the building a Latin cross shape.

The village developed around the original farmhouse and blacksmith's shop. The church was completed in 1835 and the first school buildings were constructed in 1842. The village has some 180 terraced houses. Today, the community consists of 1 720 permanent residents and 590 temporary inhabitants. All the historical buildings are provincial heritage sites.

Zuurbraak

Zuurbraak differed from the Moravian mission stations in both origin and development. It began as a Khoekhoe village under the chieftainship of *Kaptyn* (Captain) Hans Moos. In 1812 Moos obtained permission from the Cape governor, the Earl of Caledon, to invite the London Missionary Society to send a missionary to minister to his followers, among whom were a number of freed slaves. The invitation was accepted and the Society sent out a missionary by the name of Seidenfaden, who remained there until 1825.

In 1858 Governor Sir George Grey granted the farm Zuurbraak to the London Missionary Society to establish a permanent mission station. In 1873 the Society withdrew from mission work and Zuurbraak was handed over to the Dutch Reformed Church.

Pacaltsdorp

At the end of VOC rule in 1795 there were only a few independent Khoekhoe families left in the southern Cape. By 1812 the last of the independent Outeniqua had gathered at Hoogekraal, a sandy hillock situated eight kilometres south-west of present-day George. Their leader, a man the settlers referred to as 'Dikkop', appealed to visiting missionaries of the London Missionary Society to establish a mission station at Hoogekraal, as he wanted his people to be able to read and write.

In 1813 the Society sent the Reverend Charles Pacalt to Hoogekraal where he began his mission work preaching under a tree. By 1816 Pacalt had erected a small church there. In 1825 it was replaced by a stone church, built by volunteers from the community.

This church building at Zuurbraak was constructed in 1835 by the Anglican Church and was subsequently taken over by the Dutch Reformed Church.

The Pacaltsdorp stone church, with its Romanesque tower and battlemented top, was completed in 1825.

61

CHAPTER 4

The Khoe-San

DIVISION AND DEMOCRACY IN THE NINETEENTH AND TWENTIETH CENTURIES

When Sir George Napier became governor of the Cape in 1838, one of the first tasks he undertook was to consider the position of free persons of colour following slave emancipation at the end of 1834. This action was prompted by British colonial secretary Lord Glenelg, who had studied the laws of other colonies where emancipation had taken place. He came to the conclusion that 'the old Slave Code (still) exercised a very powerful influence on the structure and character'[1] of the laws affecting ex-slave communities and other persons of colour. Glenelg was determined to see that the spirit of emancipation – to which Ordinance 50 of 1828 and the abolition of slavery decree in 1833, had given effect – was not dissipated by harsh, restrictive local laws, as had happened in some colonies in the West Indies. In view of this, he sent to Napier certain Orders in Council, drafted for application in the West Indies, for guidance. Glenelg insisted that the 'principles' contained in them be upheld in the Cape as well.

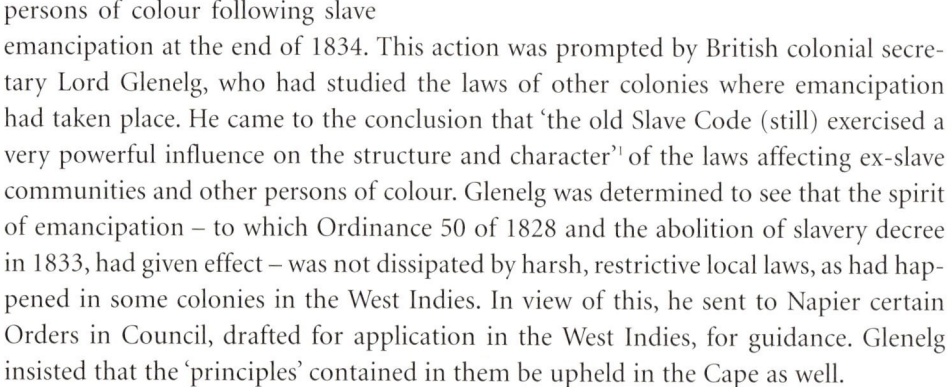

Napier found himself on the horns of a dilemma. On the one hand, he knew he had to uphold the spirit of freedom Lord Glenelg required, but, on the other, he was appalled by the extent of vagrancy in the Cape. Although the Cape governor initially wanted to tighten the laws against vagrants, he chose to promulgate a more general law after becoming more familiar with local conditions. The new Masters and Servants Ordinance 1 of 1841 was designed to revise and consolidate existing laws that protected the working class and defined the rights and duties of masters and servants. In effect, the new ordinance protected labourers against overt coercive exploitation by specifying the duration of contracts: a maximum of one year for ex-slaves and three years for Khoe-San labourers. It also required that services to be rendered and the remuneration offered had to be clearly stipulated. The ordinance was aimed at preventing the establishment of a labour system that was in any way reminiscent of slavery.

The Masters and Servants Ordinance repealed Ordinance 50 and became law in 1842, after being approved in London. It was argued that Ordinance 50 had become obsolete because it perpetuated the notion that people of colour were 'an inferior and distinct people'. The new ordinance incorporated most of the provisions of Ordinance 50, but

Increased vagrancy became a problem in the Cape after the passing of Ordinance 50 in 1828 and the emancipation of slaves after 1834. Painting by Charles Bell. (Bell Heritage Trust, UCT)

A NOTE ON NOMENCLATURE: WHO ARE THE COLOURED PEOPLE?

Equal political rights were granted to all men, regardless of colour or creed, when the Cape secured representative government in 1853. The original distinctions between the colony's inhabitants, based on origin, now no longer applied and, officially, there were no differences in privilege and status between slaves and free blacks, Khoekhoen and San. Practically, however, there remained a need for a generic and descriptive term by which all 'non-whites' could be categorised. In common with experience elsewhere in the colonial world, the term 'coloured' came into regular use.

Today, as we try to forge a common South African identity, the term 'coloured' is becoming an anachronism. But we remain burdened by the labels of the past: any attempt to be contextually and historically accurate means that the use of rather archaic terms for South Africa's people is unavoidable. In the absence of a viable alternative, the term 'coloured', or its more benevolent alternative, 'people of colour', is used in this book to describe those people in the Cape who are not Bantu-speaking and who do not have a distinct European ancestry along *both* patrilineal and matrilineal lines. In doing so, the author accepts that the term may be offensive to some readers, but hopes that the reasons for its usage are appreciated.

---

omitted those which made the Khoekhoen and other free persons of colour equal citizens before the law and which forbade the punishment of vagrancy. These clauses, it was held, had served their purpose in bringing about a new dispensation for the people of colour in the Cape and, since legal discrimination on the basis of race or colour was no longer permitted, there was no further need to make special reference to them in law. The new provisions in the Masters and Servants Ordinance were now concerned with the legal issues between employers and employees, including the effect on labour contracts of the death of either the master or the servant, insolvency, marriage, pregnancy, a change of address and the granting of testimonials. While the purpose of the ordinance was to streamline administrative procedures, its effect was 'to place the Coloured population of the Colony on a footing of complete legal equality with Europeans, and therefore to give them at last the full protection of the ordinary laws of the land. The Cape Colony ceased to know any distinction between White and Coloured people.'[2]

While it can be argued that the Masters and Servants Ordinance did have a liberal connotation, it equally had the effect of controlling the flexibility of the labour market. By laying down a code of punishment, in the form of either fines or imprisonment for both seasonal and long-term labourers who broke their contracts, the ordinance restricted labour mobility and limited the opportunities for freed slaves and Khoe-San labourers to offer their services to the highest bidder. The ordinance also failed to satisfy the farmers, who complained that it was ineffectual. In 1848 Cape Governor Sir Harry Smith instituted a commission of enquiry to examine the workings of Napier's legislation. After Britain granted representative government to the Cape in 1854, the findings were used to support the promulgation of the Masters and Servants Act of 1856, which was designed to tighten the controls that were implicit in the ordinance and to increase the severity of punishment for labourers who broke their contracts by desertion. The Act also widened the definition of offences against masters to include any refusal to obey orders. The Masters and Servants Act was a restrictive piece of legislation which remained on the statute book for 120 years until its repeal in 1974.

REPRESENTATIVE GOVERNMENT

After much lobbying by the colonists, the British Colonial Office finally agreed to the demand for representative government in the Cape. The decision had been delayed by a commission of enquiry set up by Earl Grey, the British colonial secretary. Its purpose was to investigate fears that the liberal measures which the Colonial Office had introduced in the Cape would be undone by the colonists as soon as they were given the legal means to do so. The commission found that such fears were, on the whole, groundless. This cleared the way for the adoption of a constitution in 1853, which made provision for a two-chamber parliament based on the Westminster model. In London, the newly appointed colonial secretary, the Duke of Newcastle, announced to the British parliament that 'in transmitting to the Colony of the Cape of Good Hope, ordinances which confer one of the most liberal constitutions enjoyed by any of the British possessions, Her Majesty's Government are actuated by an earnest desire to lay the foundation of institutions which may carry the blessings and privileges as well as the wealth and power of the British nation into South Africa; and whilst appeasing the jealousies of

Acting Governor Sir Charles Henry Darling opened the first Cape parliament held in the State Room of Government House on 30 June 1854. The governor, Sir George Cathcart, was not present as he had been summoned to take a command in the Crimean War. (London Illustrated News, 1854, Cape Archives)

sometimes conflicting races, to promote the security and prosperity, not only of those of British origin, but of all the Queen's subjects so that they may combine for the great common object – the peace and progress of the Colony.'[3]

The people of the Cape accepted this 'most liberal constitution' and its endorsement of the legal and political equality of all people, irrespective of the colour of their skin. With the adoption of the constitution, the 'Cape liberal tradition' became entrenched in law. In terms of the constitution, the franchise was open to all 'civilised' men. But the definition of 'civilised' was only arrived at after much acrimonious debate among the politicians. Huge disparities existed between rich and poor in the colony and the boundaries of privilege and power were traditionally drawn along racial lines. The new political dispensation required a different measure to maintain the status quo. Class, the subtle way in which many societies regulate their socio-political structures, provided that measure. It affords a stratification system based on factors such as inherited privilege, personal ownership of assets, levels of income, and control of power and privilege. It also equips politicians with a mechanism to regulate access to political power without fear of being accused of racial discrimination.

The political challenge that confronted the new legislators was to achieve consensus on the right price to be charged at the turnstiles to 'civilisation'. Entry into the 'civilised' world hinged on franchise qualifications. Argument raged on as to whether the vote should cost £25, in the form of ownership of a property worth this amount of money, or £50, in the form of annual wages. The conservatives, particularly the farmers in the north-east, wanted the highest possible qualification. The people of Cape Town were undecided: some favoured the lower franchise and a vocal few demanded the higher. Notwithstanding powerful arguments for a lower franchise, there was a general fear that it would disturb the existing equilibrium between the white minority and the black majority and alter the fulcrum of the balance of privilege in the Cape. Eventually, the higher qualification was recommended to Downing Street. The Duke of Newcastle was hesitant to accept the recommendation. Fearing widespread criticism, he hedged his bets. He restored the £25 property ownership qualification, but retained the £50 annual wage alternative proposed by the Cape Legislative Council. The Duke argued that in conferring upon the colony a representative constitution, it was

> *exceedingly undesirable that the franchise should be so restricted as to leave those of the coloured classes who, in point of intelligence, are qualified for the exercise of political power, practically unrepresented ... It is the earnest desire of Her Majesty's Government that all her subjects at the Cape without distinction of class or colour should be united by one bond of loyalty and a common interest, and we believe that the exercise of political rights enjoyed by all alike will prove one of the best methods of attaining this object.*[4]

It is interesting to note that the coloured people were never consulted about the establishment of representative government, nor did they make any formal representations on the matter. However, their silence should not be interpreted as acquiescence or disinterest. Many expected that a representative government would introduce coercive measures or recall previous legislation such as the vagrancy acts. They were also concerned about oppression by the farmers, but lacked a coordinated voice to articulate this fear. The only recorded action was that taken by forty-three people from the

Zuurbraak mission station. They told the civil commissioner at Swellendam that: 'We do not understand the proposed changes, and therefore we place our whole dependence in the Government to which we are accustomed, and under which we have lived happily and become free; we desire no change.'[5] With the unfolding of time, however, the apprehension of coloured people on the one hand and whites on the other evaporated as neither the revival of previous political oppression nor the swamping of whites by coloured and black voters occurred.

The franchise qualifications for male voters remained in force until 1892, when the urbanisation of blacks from the eastern Cape threatened to cause a stampede through the class-based turnstiles to privilege. At the instigation of the Afrikaner Bond, an organisation that represented the views of predominantly Afrikaans-speaking farmers, parliament passed the Franchise Ballot Act of 1892, which raised the franchise qualification from £25 to £75 and required each voter to prove his literacy by being able to write his name, address and occupation. The notion of 'class' was thus redefined and the price of the entry ticket into the echelons of 'civilisation' was adjusted accordingly.

THE LOOMING CRISIS

Political awareness among persons of colour in the Cape during the latter part of the nineteenth century remained at a low level. Many men who were qualified to vote did not register and no man of colour was ever nominated for election to parliament. The first coloured political party was only formed after the South African War (1899–1902). Established in 1902, it was known as the African Political Organisation and initially focused on the extension of the political rights entrenched in the Cape constitution to the defeated Boer republics across the Orange and Vaal rivers. At the time of Union in 1910, the coloured people in the Cape had only eleven per cent of the combined European and coloured votes, even though they formed forty-four per cent of the combined population. This disparity can be attributed to two principal factors. Firstly, the franchise qualification precluded a number of people from registering as voters. Secondly, there was widespread political apathy. This was partly rooted in a history of exclusion, which resulted in the coloured people being inexperienced and unfamiliar with democratic processes, partly in a general lack of education, and partly in disinterest. Allied to this, many coloured people did not consider themselves to be a separate ethnic group from whites and did not see the vote as a material factor in changing or improving their quality of life. They thus saw little need to vote. Writing of the period 1853 to 1910, L.W. Thompson noted:

> The colour line between European masters and coloured slaves and serfs had formerly created a tradition of racial discrimination. Two generations of living under free institutions gradually overcame that tradition and replaced it with a new one of tolerance, restraint and respect for the rights of the individual regardless of the colour of his skin; that is to say, the Cape liberal tradition.[6]

While critics may say that the 'Cape liberal tradition' was paternalistic, shallow and flawed, it nevertheless gave hope for a fairer world during a century when individual liberties were universally severely circumscribed. In the South African context, the Cape constitution was in sharp contrast to the constitutions of the Afrikaner republics to the north. The 1854 constitution of the Orange Free State restricted civic rights to

ABDULLAH ABDURAHMAN AND THE AFRICAN POLITICAL ORGANISATION

Abdullah Abdurahman was born in the rural town, Wellington, on 12 December 1872. From an early age it was obvious that he was destined for big things. Despite the disadvantage of colour, his vision, drive, academic ability and single-minded determination to succeed resulted in him graduating, in 1893, at the age of twenty-one, as a medical doctor from the University of Glasgow.

In 1904 Abdurahman became the first black person to be elected to the Cape Town City Council. Initially some councillors ostracised him, refusing to sit next to him or even to acknowledge him. Abdurahman was not intimidated. His personal charm, political acumen, good oratory and skilled negotiation won them over, and he retained a seat on the council until his death in 1940. A decade after joining the city council, Abdurahman was elected to the Cape Provincial Council, a position he held for the rest of his life. Importantly, he enjoyed extensive support among coloured voters and this gave him considerable leverage in his cause to promote coloured political interests throughout South Africa.

Abdurahman rose to national prominence in the aftermath of the South African War. Driven by a philosophy that all citizens should be equal before the law and that the franchise be colour-blind, he foresaw that the unification of the colonies and the former boer republics was likely to have adverse consequences for the coloured community. He realised that the Cape's liberal tradition was at odds with the conservative, segregationist policies of the former Boer republics, and so he set about ensuring that coloured rights in the Cape would not be tampered with and advocating that the same rights should be extended to the other provinces as well.

The first substantive coloured political organisation, the African Political Organisation (APO) was founded in 1902 to articulate the aspirations of coloured people and to mobilise them to promote the extension of coloured rights in Natal, Transvaal and the Orange Free State. Abdurahman joined the APO in 1903. Two years later he became its president, a position he would hold for the next thirty-five years. Under his leadership, the APO developed from a highly factional body into the largest black political organisation in the country in the early twentieth century. By 1910 it had several thousand paid-up members and a national network of over a hundred branches. During the next thirty years the APO remained a significant coloured political organisation, not only dominating coloured protest politics, but also mobilising and coordinating initiatives aimed at uplifting the socio-economic conditions of the coloured community.

Between 1906 and 1910 the APO campaigned tirelessly for Britain to veto any attempts to deny coloured people voting rights in the national realignment of political structures in South Africa. Later, in the 1920s and 1930s, as the tide of Afrikaner Nationalism began to rise, Abdurahman led APO campaigns against government initiatives to undermine the economic and political status of coloured people and entered into pacts with those white parties that were likely to serve coloured interests best.

While Abdurahman's prime interest was the advancement of the coloured community, he recognised the need for unity within the broader black political community to counter white political supremacism. Between 1927 and 1934 he jointly convened with D.D.T. Jabavu of the Cape Native Voters' Convention four conferences of black political organisations, but nothing significant came of these because of organisational rivalries and personal jealousies. In 1925 he was requested by the South African Indian Congress to lead a delegation to the Indian government to seek assistance in preventing the Union government from passing anti-Indian legislation. This led to a series of round-table conferences between the two governments.

It was in the field of educational reform that Abdurahman probably achieved his best results. He recognised that the sort of society he wanted to create would not be possible as long as coloured children had unequal access to education. The vastly inferior church schools, which provided the only schooling for coloured children, simply did not have sufficient resources, and the improvement of educational facilities was thus one of his most important goals. He took the lead in establishing Trafalgar High School (1911) and Livingstone High School (1934) – the first two secondary schools to be established for coloured students in Cape Town.

In 1913 he initiated the establishment of the Teachers' League of South Africa, which later played a key role in coloured education reform.

Abdurahman's critics dismissed him as an opportunist and a collaborator. In his quest for the steady assimilation of the coloured community into the white community on the basis of the old Cape liberal tradition, his critics saw capitulation. And in his inability to deliver tangible benefits on a national scale in the face of increasing white minority intransigence, they saw the failure of the liberal values he espoused. Over time, black opposition to government policies became more radical, and Abdurahman's liberal legacy was temporarily forgotten. However, by the end of the twentieth century, the liberal values of personal freedom and non-racial democracy that he espoused were enshrined in the constitution of the new South Africa. In recognition of the role that Abdurahman played in the development of democracy in South Africa, one of the last official duties Nelson Mandela performed as President of South Africa was to posthumously award him the Order for Meritorious Service: Class I (Gold) in June 1999. A fitting tribute to a talented man.

burghers, who could only be 'white persons'. In terms of another Orange Free State law, no 'Arab, Chinaman or Coolie or other Asiatic or Coloured person' could settle in the republic or even remain there for longer than two months without official permission. The constitution of the Zuid Afrikaansche Republiek (ZAR) stated that 'the people [burghers] desire to permit no equality between Coloured people and the White inhabitants, either in Church or State.'

In the aftermath of the South African War, representatives from the Cape, Natal, Free State and Transvaal gathered to discuss the establishment of a Union with a single national government. The National Convention began its sittings in 1908, and one of the most contentious issues it faced was the proposal by the Cape delegation to extend the franchise to all citizens, irrespective of race or colour. Colonel Stanford told the delegates that '[a]ll subjects of Her Majesty resident in South Africa shall be entitled to franchise rights irrespective of race or colour upon such qualifications as may be determined by this Convention.'[7] He was supported by J.W. Sauer, who declared that:

> If the delegates from the Cape advocated the Cape system it was because they spoke from experience and their experience was satisfactory … If they were to have a contented country the interests of all must be represented in the Parliament of the country

and there must be political equality ... The great principle of justice was at stake in this discussion and there must be a just native policy or the white man would go under in South Africa. Justice could not be tampered with impunity and justice to the native would secure the position of the white man in South Africa for all time.[8]

In stark contrast, the former Boer republics opposed the notion of equality between blacks and whites. General Koos de la Rey warned that the Cape policy had been a 'dangerous mistake, and might if they were not careful lead to trouble in South Africa ... It was an essential thing that the white races should unite in South Africa and they must not allow this coloured question to prevent that Union.'[9] Eventually a compromise was reached, and it was agreed that the Convention would 'leave the position in the Cape as it now stands and allow the Union Parliament to settle the question at some future date'.[10]

The compromise came at a price, though. The South Africa Act, which came into effect on 31 May 1910, effectively excluded blacks from registering as voters, although people of colour in the Cape retained their franchise rights. It also stipulated that only British subjects of European descent could sit in parliament. There was, however, one concession that the men from the South had won, namely, the right of parliament to extend the Cape franchise to the rest of South Africa. It was hoped that in time an open franchise would become a nationally accepted norm. The reverse was to happen.

Co-founder of the National Party in 1914, James Barry Munnik Hertzog served as prime minister of South Africa between 1924 and 1939.

A PRECARIOUS HONEYMOON AND PAINFUL DIVORCE

The period between 1910 and 1948 was a precarious one for people of colour, who had a limited say in the running of their country. Coloured men in the Cape province had the franchise, but they could not vote for a person of colour to represent them in parliament. Paradoxically, it was not the intention of the early segregationists to exclude coloured people from political processes in the country. General J.B.M. Hertzog, founder of the National Party of South Africa and prime minister from 1924 to 1939, defined his party's policy in respect of the coloured people:

In this respect we have to remember that we have to do with a section of the community closely allied to the white population, and one that is fundamentally different from the natives. He owes his origin to us and knows no other civilisation than that of the European ... and even speaks the language of the European as his mother tongue. There can thus be no talk of segregation. That is the reason why, during the past seven years, the Nationalists in Parliament have held the view that the Cape Coloured people must be treated on an equality [sic] *with Europeans – economically, industrially and politically.*[11]

When Dr Daniël François Malan was Minister of the Interior in Hertzog's cabinet, he also advocated equal political rights for people of colour. In June 1925 he stated that the government 'is making sure that there shall be no colour bar for the Coloured person and for the Malays.'[12] In a booklet outlining his political views, entitled *Die Groot Vlug*, Malan pleaded for the inclusion of equal rights for all coloured people:

> *The Coloured has adopted the white man's civilisation. He dresses the same way and eats the same food as the European, lives in a brick house too, also supports his Church and sends his children to school. Segregation of the Coloureds is not only impossible but also unnecessary. With the degree of civilisation they have already acquired, they are no danger to the European.*[13]

South African politics has a history of enigma and unpredictability. In 1934 D.F. Malan broke away from Hertzog's National Party to form the *Gesuiwerde* (Purified) National Party. In the same year, Hertzog and General Jan Smuts joined forces to launch the United South African National Party and Malan became the new Leader of the Opposition. One of the fundamental differences that emerged between Hertzog and Malan concerned the political separation of the races in South Africa. Malan's fear was that if whites had to open the race gate even slightly to allow coloured voters to trickle through, they would not be able to shut it against a rising tide of qualified African voters. As a result, Malan did a complete political volte-face. With an eye on increasing urbanisation and the rising tide of black politics, he now argued that the gate should be kept tightly shut and advocated a rigid separation of all race groups. Hertzog, on the other hand, felt that the separation between Europeans and Africans was 'sufficient to guarantee the continued existence of the White man in South Africa',[14] while that between whites and coloureds should be minimised.

Malan made his views clear in a party manifesto released in Porterville on 4 April 1938. The manifesto rescinded his past assurances that the colour line lay between Europeans and coloureds on one side and Africans on the other. Instead, he advocated that it be drawn between Europeans and non-Europeans (everybody who was not a direct descendant of pure-blooded European parentage). The ideal of total segregation as the political solution to South Africa's race problems gained much of its emotional appeal from the gathering strength of Afrikaner Nationalism, which fed on a history of discontent and the fear among whites of being swamped by the black people of Africa. Thus, apartheid and Afrikaner Nationalism began to walk hand in hand along the same road to a common destiny. One of the many casualties that lay *en route* was the coloured franchise, a right, albeit qualified, that the Cape's people of colour shared with their white counterparts for almost a century. Apartheid required that the two be separated.

General Jan Christiaan Smuts, prime minister between 1919 and 1924 and between 1939 and 1940, international statesman, brilliant scholar and philosopher, and world-renowned amateur botanist, failed to appreciate the full significance of South Africa's multiracial composition. He thus did not offer white voters a political vision which could counter D.F. Malan's pernicious promise of apartheid.

The divorce was acrimonious and was fought bitterly in parliament and in the courts. But the Nationalist government, driven by the need to draw impenetrable boundaries around race and to restrict access to privilege and power, was determined to disenfranchise coloured voters. Its attempts to repeal Section 35 of the South Africa Act, which provided for the coloured vote, and to pass the Separate Representation of Voters Act met with fierce opposition from within and outside parliament. However, the government would stop at nothing, not even the rigging of parliament, to achieve its objective. By pushing through the Senate Act of 1956, with the backing of a restructured Appellate Division, the Nationalists managed to increase the number of elected senators. In February 1956, a packed parliament passed, with a majority of 174 votes to 68, the Separate Representation of Voters Amendment Act. The law was challenged in the courts, but the Appellate Division judges, with the exception of one dissenting voice, ensured that it was upheld.

Dr Daniël François Malan (1874–1959)

Dr Daniël François Malan, accompanied by his wife, Maria, attends the opening of parliament on 24 January 1953. This was to be his last year in parliament and his last attempt to remove coloured voters from the common voters' roll. He failed, and the task fell to his successor, J.G. Strijdom. In 1956 parliament passed the Separate Representation of Voters Amendment Act, which made provision for a separate roll for coloured voters.

Daniël François Malan was born near Riebeeck West on 22 May 1874 and died at Stellenbosch on 7 February 1959. He was in his mid-twenties when the Boer republics went to war with the British in 1899. As a Dutch Reformed minister in Montagu and later in Graaff-Reinet, he experienced firsthand the despair, hopelessness and trauma of the defeated Afrikaners. He resolved to make it his life's work to restore a sense of dignity and self-worth to the Afrikaner people, so that they could take what he saw to be their rightful place as an equal nation in South Africa.

He left the church and took up politics, eventually becoming the father of Afrikaner Nationalism and, as South Africa's fourth premier, the ideological founder of the official policy of post-war apartheid. In the process, the coloured people, whom Malan once fully embraced because their 'interests and those of the whites are the same and [they] will use [their] vote properly',[15] were ideologically sacrificed on the altar of apartheid. Their colour was now wrong and this meant that they would no longer 'vote properly'.

A protracted and acrimonious political battle was waged in the first half of the twentieth century to save the coloured vote. Eventually the Nationalists got their way and the coloured people lost their more than a century-old right to vote for members of first the Cape parliament and then the South African parliament.

THE ADVENT OF DEMOCRACY

The National Party gained a pyrrhic victory. The cost was a half century of escalating bitterness and disillusionment among coloured people and their increasing alienation from whites with whom they once shared equal voting rights on a common roll. For over four decades the Nationalist government steadfastly implemented its policy of apartheid through the creation of various institutions of government and the application of numerous statutory and administrative measures to separate the coloured community from the white community in all spheres of life. But try as it might, it could not unscramble the South African human omelette and eventually it had to capitulate. When universal suffrage and democratic government came to the country in 1994, the Cape's people of colour regained their rightful place as equal citizens in the land of their birth.

Despite the attainment of political equality, the country's coloured people have inherited a legacy of economic disadvantage – the result of being the descendants of dispossessed San hunter-gathers, Khoekhoe herders, slaves, and the progeny of interracial unions in a country that attached privilege to the whiteness of a person's skin. It will take much wisdom and time to redress the alienation coloured people have experienced in the wake of colonialism and racism. But before a sustained momentum in the process of growth, change and reconciliation can be achieved, it is necessary to restore the qualities that colonialism took away: dignity, self-worth and personal empowerment.

CHAPTER 5

The Khoe-San

DIGNITY, SELF-WORTH AND ASPIRATIONS

We have seen how the colonists treated the San as they spread out from Cape Town – first as an obstacle and then as vermin to be shot on sight. We have seen how the Khoekhoen steadily lost access to the land and its resources and then, with the exception of the Griqua, gave up the struggle to maintain their herding lifestyle and became labourers. We have seen how Ordinance 50 of 1828 gave the Khoekhoen some measure of reprieve, how the emancipation of slaves in 1834 and the abolition of the apprenticeship system in 1838 gave slaves their freedom, and how the Cape's 'most liberal constitution' gave coloured men equal political rights. Despite these measures, the coloured community as a whole remained on the lower rungs of the socio-economic ladder. It is a sad but accurate reflection that this is where the majority still are today, in spite of nearly ten years of democratic government. There are two principal reasons for this. The first is an historical distortion in the ownership of resources which has resulted in an economic system that has favoured the 'haves' at the expense of the 'have-nots'. The second is the deep-seated psychological damage, manifested in feelings of personal and community inferiority, caused by a long history of master-and-servant social relations and a racially based class structure entrenched by law and custom.

The democratic institutions of the new South Africa are dealing with the physical impediments to personal and community economic growth. But the psychological factors restraining personal and community development are far more problematic and difficult to resolve. To begin with, the deeply-felt wrongs of the past need to be adequately addressed so that the roots that nourish feelings of inferiority and low self-esteem can be extracted and allowed to wither and die. Without a sense of self-worth, real personal and economic empowerment is only a mirage, and mirages destroy morale and inevitably take away hope. Breaking this cycle is one of South Africa's greatest challenges. To meet it, it is necessary to expurgate not only the many laws that entrenched racially based privilege, but also the attitudes of racial superiority that underpinned those laws and which continue to mould dangerous and debilitating stereotypes.

Many descendants of the Cape's indigenous people continue to occupy the lower rungs of Cape society as a result of an historical imbalance in the ownership and distribution of resources.

EARLY SCIENCE AND RACIAL SUPERIORITY

The historical evidence of attitudes of racial superiority is to be found not only in laws and the traditional relationships that existed between masters and servants, but also in the classification of people by early scientists. The preoccupation with classifying southern Africa's people is seen in the large anthropological collections of Khoe-San remains that have intrigued both European and South African scientists for many years. In attempting to understand this obsession, social scientist Alan Morris argues that

> part of the fascination stems from the nature of colonial rule. The colonisers separated humanity in the metropole from humanity in the colony. 'Civilised' people were above nature, while the 'primitives' in the colony were members of the animal kingdom to be classified and listed amongst the weird and wonderful fauna of distant lands.[1]

Some scholars in Europe considered the Khoekhoen and the San to have been less than human. Some even claimed that the San constituted a side-branch of the human family. Tobias points out that many of these claims were based on pelvic and genital observations.[2] Driven by the need to classify all forms of life, Swedish naturalist Carolus Linnaeus, who toured the Cape in 1735, viewed the Khoekhoen and the San as completely separate species to *Homo sapiens sapiens*. Eugene Marais, the well-known South African poet, writer and naturalist, who did pioneering scientific work on baboon behaviour in the early twentieth century, could not accept that the San were part of the human race. He believed that the 'profound somatic differences between the Bushman and the lowest human race precludes all idea of a common species ... Everything points to a near ape-ancestry and to an ape-ancestry different from that of the rest of the human race.'[3] Even as recently as 1913, the Cape Synod of the Dutch Reformed Church, which had been in existence for 250 years, 'had an intense debate on whether the Bushmen should be seen as human beings or animals.'[4]

The view that the Khoe-San were less than human was apparent in the public display in Europe of some Khoe-San people with unusual physical features. There they were gawked at as items of curiosity, amusement and derision. One example of such a person was Sarah Bartmann, a young Khoekhoe woman from the Cape. Sarah was born in the Gamtoos Valley in the eastern Cape in 1789 and later moved with her parents to Cape Town. When she was twenty years old, she was employed as a domestic servant by a farmer, Peter Cezar, whose brother, Hendrik, was married to Sarah. Alexander Dunlop, a visiting English ship's doctor who had been staying on Cezar's farm, became intrigued with Sarah's pronounced buttocks and genitalia. He persuaded her to sail with him to England, promising her fame and riches if she agreed to display her body in public.

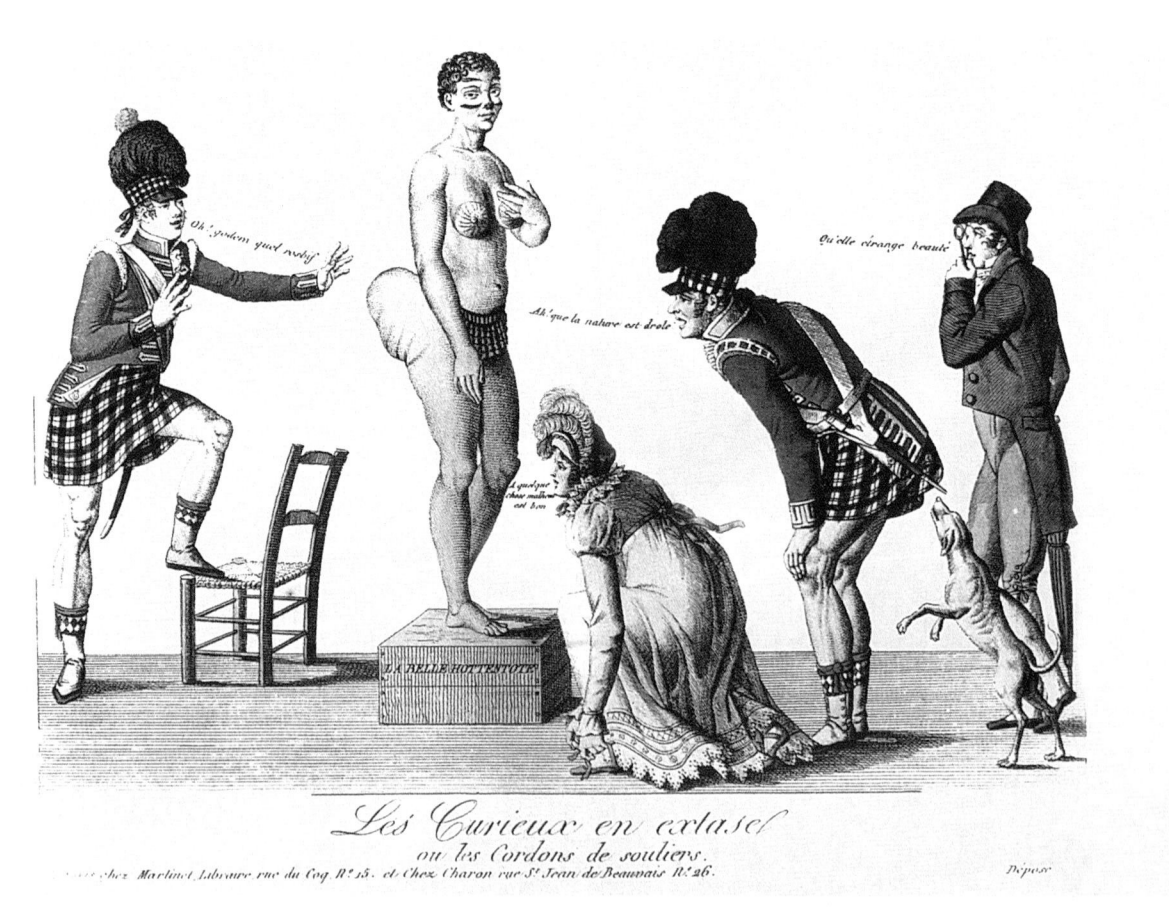

Sarah Bartmann's pose depicted in this early nineteenth-century engraving is an obvious parody of Sandro Botticelli's Birth of Venus *(c. 1485). The mockery continues in the illustration of the viewers' curiosity, the inscription on the plinth,* La Belle Hottentote, *and the burlesque title of the engraving,* The Curious in Ecstasy at the Shoelaces.

EARLY SCIENCE AND RACIAL SUPERIORITY

Whether Sarah really understood what she was letting herself in for is a matter of conjecture and debate. On arriving in Europe, she became the subject of close anatomical scrutiny by scientists who referred to her genitalia as the 'Hottentot apron'. She was advertised as the 'Hottentot Venus', a grotesque parody of Botticelli's *Birth of Venus*. At Piccadilly people paid one shilling and queued to view her perceived grotesqueness, difference and racial inferiority. She was taken to circuses, museums, bars and universities where she was required to exhibit her physical features. At times she was caged, creating the effect of her being a wild animal. At the request of scientist Étienne Geoffroy Saint-Hilaire, she was taken to France for scientific research, the findings of which became the bedrock of European ideas about black sexuality. In Paris she was paraded before a French public eager to see a representative of what was billed as a 'subhuman' species from Africa.

In 1815, at the age of 27, Sarah Bartmann died, possibly from pneumonia. Her body was taken to the Musée de l'Homme where scientist Georges Cuvier dissected it. He made a plaster cast of her body, preserved her brain and genitals in glass jars, and exhibited her skeleton in the museum. Even in death the young Khoekhoe woman was used to 'titillate' visitors. She remained on display until 1975, when public pressure forced the French authorities to remove her remains from the museum's shelves. Two years after Sarah's death, Cuvier published an article entitled 'Observations on the body of a woman well-known in Paris and London under the name of Hottentot Venus', in which he claimed that races with depressed and compressed skulls were condemned to a never-ending inferiority. This reinforced the assumption among European scientists that racial superiority and racial inferiority were related to physical characteristics.

Following the first democratic election in South Africa in 1994, there was a strong feeling that Sarah Bartmann should be brought home. After lengthy negotiations between the South African and French governments, her remains were returned to the country in 2002.

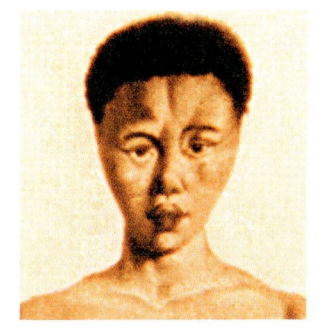

Drawn from life, this image of Sarah Bartmann is part of a nineteenth-century lithograph called Femme de Race Boschmann (Bushman woman). *It was published in 1824 by scientists Étienne Geoffroy Saint-Hilaire and Georges Cuvier in a joint paper entitled,* 'Histoire Naturelle des Mammifères' *('Natural history of mammals').*

Below: Sarah Bartmann's final resting place at Hankey in the Eastern Cape.

THE RETURN OF SARAH BARTMANN

Sarah Bartmann's return to Africa, to the place of her birth and her people, became an imperative for the new South Africa. In achieving this goal, the Griqua National Conference of South Africa took the lead.

On 6 December 1995 the Conference delivered a Protest Note to the French Embassy in Pretoria, calling for the 'surrender to the autochtonous, aboriginal and indigenous GRIQUA, in their capacity as a *First Nation* of South Africa and as guardians and custodians of continuous, uninterrupted and unbroken Cape aboriginal Khoikhoi heritage, language and identity, the remains of the late Miss Sarah Bartmann (*alias Saartjie Baartman*) for appropriate burial in her native land, and the consequent, but belated, restitution of her dignity and that of the aboriginal Khoikhoi and their descendants, the Griqua.'

It took seven years of intensive negotiation at governmental and non-governmental levels and a special Act passed in the French National Assembly to have Sarah's remains released from the Musée de l'Homme in Paris and returned to South Africa.

As a woman, deeply humiliated as a result of racial misconceptions, her dignity had to be symbolically restored. As an icon of South Africa's indigenous people, her continuous humiliation was a humiliation to all her people. The slate of indignity thus had to be wiped clean. To do so, Sarah Bartmann had to return to her homeland, and her remains had to be enrobed according to Khoekhoe custom and laid to rest among her people in a proper grave in the Eastern Cape, surrounded by the hills, trees and grasses she once knew.

Sarah Bartmann's return and proper burial were important milestones in the attempt to loosen the vice of a past predicated on beliefs of inherited racial inferiority.

A special ceremony to enrobe the remains of Sarah Bartmann was held in Cape Town prior to her burial on 9 August 2002. The event played an important role in symbolically restoring the dignity of both Sarah and the country's Khoe-San people. The public ceremony, addressed by ex-Deputy Minister of Arts, Culture, Science and Technology Brigitte Mabandla (top), celebrated her memory through poetry, song and the burning of traditional kooigoed *(selected herbs).*

REBUILDING THE PAST

Allied to the process of removing the stain of racial disdain that has disfigured the social fabric of South African society for so long is the recognition of the heritage bequeathed to us by the Cape's indigenous people. Of paramount importance in this regard are San rock paintings and engravings, a profoundly spiritual art tradition filled with complex symbols and metaphors. The rock art of southern Africa is a unique heritage, unequalled anywhere else in the world. As such, it deserves to be protected and cherished.

Writers have pointed to the role San imagery can play in the shaping of a new South African national identity. They see the San as offering a bridge between the past and the future and they seek to promote the concept of 'San' as a motivation for reconciliation between divided communities. In this regard, it is significant to note that the motto on South Africa's new coat of arms, unveiled by President Thabo Mbeki on 27 April 2002, is !ke e: /xarra //ke. Taken from /Xam, an extinct San language, it literally means 'people who are different join together'. On the centre shield are two human figures derived from images on the Linton stone, a world-famous example of South African rock art, now housed in the Iziko: South African Museum in Cape Town. The two San figures are depicted in an attitude of greeting, which symbolises unity. The image represents the beginning of the individual's transformation, leading to his or her greater sense of belonging to the nation and, by extension, collective humanity. San rock art, South Africa's oldest heritage, is thus at the forefront of the nation's new identity:

The San figures in the national coat of arms symbolise unity.

> The heritage survives to this day in the rocky recesses and outcrops across the country and, as one of the most vivid and enduring works of prehistoric culture, it tells of South Africa's unbroken past, its predicaments and glories. Undoubtedly, it can restore the integrity of indigenous history and promote a common sense of nationhood. Rock art opens a vista onto the past that goes beyond the notorious apartheid idea that there was no history in this country before 1652.[5]

The rock art left by South Africa's first people is a national treasure, and is a potent symbol in forging a common sense of nationhood.

Indigenous knowledge systems passed down from the Cape's first people to the present are an important and valuable heritage, not only in terms of culture but also in terms of economics. For example, the commercial use of indigenous plants, roots and shrubs, especially for food and medicinal purposes, is bringing economic relief to many people living in poverty-stricken rural areas. The medicinal benefits of buchu (*Agathosma* sp.) were first discovered by the San, and today the oil extracted from the plant sells for between R3 000 and R9 000 a litre. An extract made from several species of *Hoodia*, originally used as an appetite and thirst suppressant by the San, provides the

Rooibos tea is made from the indigenous shrub Aspalathus linearis. *This example of a rooibos plant is on a farm in the Clanwilliam district in the Western Cape.*

raw material for an anti-obesity drug that has a market potential worth billions of rands. Several species of honeybush (*Cyclopia* spp.) have been used for centuries by the Khoe-San living in the Langeberg to make a refreshing tea. Today, honeybush tea is being exported to the United States of America and other countries around the globe. The same applies to rooibos tea, an established herbal drink made from *Aspalathus linearis*.

PROMOTING KHOE-SAN INTERESTS

In rebuilding the past, the promotion of Khoe-San identity and cultural heritage is being undertaken at a number of levels. The first level is that of awareness creation. Significantly, Tobias notes that it is 'only fairly recently that "Khoisan" [Khoe-San] has resurfaced in South Africa'.[6] The use of the word 'resurfaced' is relevant. Although assimilation and a considerable amount of cultural loss have taken place over the last 350 years, the relevance of 'indigenousness' has become much more pronounced with the advent of democracy in South Africa than it was during colonial and apartheid times when there was a stigma attached to being indigenous. Today, being indigenous is seen by many as evoking a sense of pride and giving substance to the heritage left by those who lived on the subcontinent thousands of years before Jan van Riebeeck landed at the Cape. Being indigenous also provides the opportunity to negate the insult implied in the generic term 'coloured', which, in its broadest sense, insinuates amorphousness and the lack of cultural roots and identity. Since 1995 several initiatives have been launched to promote an awareness of the importance of being Khoe-San, to explore Khoe-San identity, and to uncover the roots that will nourish cultural pride, growth and development.

At a second level, a comprehensive strategy is being developed for sustainable cultural growth and development and to coordinate numerous multifaceted Khoe-San endeavours. To begin the process, a national Khoisan Consultative Conference, initiated by the Institute for Historical Research at the University of the Western Cape, was held in Oudtshoorn in 2001. The intention of the conference was to bring together in a single forum thirty-four different Khoe-San organisations. Pertinent issues were examined, including religious values, culture and identity, economic empowerment, international affiliation, the involvement of women, intellectual property rights and indigenous knowledge systems. Land rights, the constitutional accommodation of Khoe-San rights and a national Khoisan Legacy Project were also discussed. At the end of the conference, a committee was established, a programme of action was drawn up and milestones were identified against which progress could be measured.

A number of national organisations have come into being to promote Khoe-San interests and welfare. The oldest of these is the Griqua National Conference of South Africa. Established by Griqua chief and prophet Andrew Abraham Stockenstrom Le Fleur I in 1904 on the Cape Flats in Cape Town, it had several objectives: to mobilise and reunite Griqua descendants into an identifiable unit and simultaneously to reject the notion of being 'coloured'; to resist the carrying of passes; and to heed the instructions God revealed to Le Fleur from time to time. One of the Griqua nation's most significant heritage projects today is the Ratelgat Development Trust Project, established on traditional land near Vanrhynsdorp. It was at Ratelgat that Le Fleur made most of his important prophecies.

THE GRIQUA RATELGAT DEVELOPMENT TRUST PROJECT

On 2 July 1933, the day of his birthday, Griqua chief Andrew Abraham Stockenstrom Le Fleur I, known to his followers as the *Kneg* (the servant of God), declared, perhaps on an impulse, perhaps on divine inspiration, that he was relocating from the Griqua settlement at Beeswater in the Vredendal district to Luiperskop, a sheep farm on the Knersvlakte about fifty kilometres distant.

After a lease had been negotiated, the *Kneg* left for Luiperskop, urging his followers to join him whenever they could. When the *Kneg* arrived at the farm, he established his first camp near a waterhole which he found by following the wet tracks of a *ratel* (badger). In gratitude, he called the farm Ratelgat (badger hole).

Le Fleur later moved his camp to a low rise, Peperneus, with a commanding view across the undulating semi-desert plains that stretched out before it. There he and his followers built their *matjieshuise*, using sacking to clad the frames. A number of projects were initiated to provide the Griqua people with work and a source of income. These included extracting coloured powders from various clays to use as pigments in paint; prospecting for minerals; curing lime from locally extracted rock; and planting hardy trees, for example wild tobacco (*Nicotiana glauca*), whose leaves, warmed over a fire, were used as painkillers. The Griqua also attempted to establish agricultural projects, but the saline content of the soil and irregular rainfall in the region prevented these from getting off the ground.

It was at Ratelgat that the *Kneg* found comfort and peace and where he received his most important instructions from God and delivered many of his prophecies. As a result, Ratelgat has a special spiritual significance for the Griqua. To commemorate this and to honour the *Kneg*, a memorial was built at the place where the Griqua leader lived during his last years at Ratelgat.

On 1 May 1999 the former Minister of Agriculture and Land Affairs, Derek Hanekom, handed over the farm Luiperskop to the Griqua Ratelgat Development Trust, comprising eighty-five trustees who could trace residential connections to Ratelgat. In this historic act of land restitution, another of Le Fleur's prophecies – that the Griqua would acquire Ratelgat at no cost to themselves – came to pass. Today, Ratelgat provides an opportunity for the Griqua to put into practice the *Kneg*'s

This lime kiln at Ratelgat was built by the Kneg *in the 1930s to produce an income for the Griqua.*

vision of economic self-sufficiency. Throughout his life the *Kneg* emphasised the need for the Griqua to own and develop their own land in order to generate a sustainable income, thereby lifting themselves out of poverty.

With the help of consultants, the Griqua National Conference has designed a sustainable four-nodal development plan for Ratelgat. The first node, near the entrance gate, will comprise a tourist complex made up of a living cultural centre, an arts and crafts display, a conference facility, an indigenous succulent nursery and a tourist information bureau. The second node will comprise a twelve-chalet rest camp. The third node, based at the *Kneg* memorial, will include an amphitheatre. The eastern part of the farm constitutes the fourth node and the area has been earmarked for a camping site and small observatory. Sheep will also be reared and kept on different parts of the farm for commercial purposes.

The dream for Ratelgat is that it should be a place of spiritual renewal that is also financially viable and sustainable. As an example of both a successful land restitution project and a creative cultural initiative, Ratelgat provides a powerful stimulus for reconciliation. As an account of Griqua and Khoekhoe history, culture and indigenous knowledge systems, it promotes understanding and respect. Finally, it serves as a didactic model for sustainable development, and could be replicated elsewhere.

This memorial at Ratelgat near Vanrhynsdorp was erected by the Griqua National Conference in honour of former Griqua chief Andrew Abraham Stockenstrom Le Fleur I (the Kneg*).*

CAN THE GRIQUA CLAIM FIRST PEOPLE STATUS?

In some circles the question has been raised of whether the Griqua qualify for the status of first people. Social scientist Alan Morris has researched the biological and historical origins of the Griqua in the eighteenth and nineteenth centuries. In a paper, 'The Griqua and the Khoikhoi: Biology, ethnicity and the construction of identity', delivered at the Khoisan Identities and Cultural Heritage Conference in Cape Town in 1997, he examines the development of the Griqua as a heterogeneous but distinct society. He argues that 'although the Khoikhoi have made up a significant portion of this ancestry, claims for "historical continuity" with the Khoikhoi are exaggerated and that the Griqua better represent a union of diversity rather than a repository of purity'.[8] He points out that their biological history 'suggests a multi-origin group which has developed as a heterogeneous but distinct society which encompasses a substantial biological and cultural input from the aboriginal Khoikhoi'.[9] However, as to the question of whether the Griqua can be described as aboriginal, his answer is an unequivocal yes:

The formation of the Griqua is a specifically South African event in which a new population has been moulded with its own distinctive political, ethnic and biological history. The identity of the Griqua does not depend on the specific Khoikhoi origins of the group, but instead on its special history as identifiable political and social communities.[10]

The Griqua National Conference is open to all Griqua and other Khoekhoe descendants. It is an effective and well-structured organisation, with branches in the Western Cape, Northern Cape, Free State and Eastern Cape. The Conference advocates self-determination for the Griqua based on a definition of aboriginality which incorporates criteria such as the use of traditional lands, historical continuity and cultural distinctiveness. Pursuant to the acknowledgement of self-determination, the Conference demands 'representation at all levels of government; traditional leadership-status; the restitution of violated treaties; the return of all Griqua land usurped by colonial powers but now inherited illegally by the nation-state of South Africa; and compensation for untold suffering, genocide and ethnocide inflicted on the Griqua and their Khoisan ancestors as culturally, linguistically, socially, economically and politically deprived, disempowered and decimated aboriginal, autochthonous and indigenous people of southern Africa.'[7]

The National Khoi-San Council was established by the South African government in 2001 to provide an official, all-inclusive consultative mechanism through which constitutional accommodation of the Khoe-San can be negotiated. Another organisation, the National Council of Khoi Chiefs, has set itself the task of resurrecting historically accurate traditional leadership structures among those Khoekhoe groups that disbanded during the colonial era and whose members became physically dispersed. It has assumed the responsibility for inducting suitable persons as chiefs in a culturally acceptable way that accords with traditional practices.

At a third level, a number of non-governmental organisations have been created with the specific purpose of facilitating the protection of San culture and heritage. An important roleplayer in this field is the Working Group for Indigenous Minorities of Southern Africa (WIMSA). The organisation was established in 1996, at the request of the San in South Africa, Botswana and Namibia, to serve as a platform to discuss their respective problems, needs and concerns. WIMSA has a regional office in Windhoek, Namibia, which coordinates efforts around San issues for the entire southern African region. Its main tasks are to advocate and lobby for San rights and to support a network it had helped to establish for information exchange among its twenty-four San member organisations and eleven support organisations. The support organisations, based in Europe, America and Africa, provide professional expertise and logistical support to WIMSA when necessary.

In response to a need expressed by WIMSA, the South African San Institute (SASI) was founded in 1996. Its purpose is to create multidisciplinary development projects in fields such as education, leadership training, capacity building, intellectual property rights, land rights, cultural resources management, oral history collection and community mobilisation. It collaborates with non-governmental organisations and government agencies to implement projects and participates in various sectoral networks. An important project in which SASI is involved is the !Khwa ttu San Culture and Education Centre near Yzerfontein on the west coast. It is currently being developed as a cultural tourism and heritage centre and serves as a training facility for the San.

SASI has played a significant role in the San's battle for the restitution of their traditional land. In the only current example of a successful aboriginal land claim in southern Africa, the ≠Khomani San gained control over 65 000 hectares of land in the Northern Cape. In the first phase 38 000 hectares of farmland situated around the confluence of the Molopo and Nossob rivers, approximately fifty kilometres south of the Kgalagadi Transfrontier Park, were handed over to the ≠Khomani San. The second phase comprised the transfer of 28 000 hectares within the Park itself, which will be jointly managed by the South African National Parks Board and the San.

SASI is also facilitating the reclaiming of San languages thought to have died out during the colonial and apartheid eras. One of the criteria used to determine indigenous rights, including land restitution rights, is indigenous identity. An important mechanism for establishing this is oral history. In the ≠Khomani San land claim, the revival of oral history and indigenous languages played an essential part in establishing the aboriginal identity of the claimants.

A member of the ≠Khomani San group making curios to sell to tourists passing to and from the Kgalagadi Transfrontier Park. This sort of activity not only generates a much-needed income for San communities, but also has a positive impact on their cultural revival as it stimulates an interest among the San in their own artefacts and heritage.

!KHWA TTU SAN CULTURE AND EDUCATION CENTRE

A renovated farm building serves as a training centre, one of several facilities established at the !Khwa ttu Culture and Education Centre.

The !Khwa ttu Centre, located on an 850-hectare farm near Yzerfontein some seventy kilometres north of Cape Town, is a celebration of San heritage and culture. The farm was originally known as Grootwater (Big Water), but was renamed !Khwa ttu, meaning 'water pans' in the /Xam language.

A San cultural tourism and development project, the !Khwa ttu Centre is facilitated by the Working Group for Indigenous Minorities of Southern Africa. Its aims are:
- to bring back to the Western Cape the heritage of the San as expressed in their culture, history, folklore, visual arts, cosmology and language
- to stimulate a greater awareness and knowledge of the San within the broader South African society
- to provide training to the San in general and income-generating skills, including entrepreneurship, construction work, tourism, community development, craft production, marketing, health and gender issues
- to ensure that the San themselves benefit directly from an increasing number of ecotourism, filmmaking and advertising initiatives that have developed around them.

Several historical buildings on the farm have been renovated by San trainee builders. Plans are afoot to use the buildings for a multimedia San museum, a rock art information centre, an arts and crafts studio and guest facilities.

San trainees are also involved in efforts to restore the land. San heritage is closely associated with the natural environment and the reintegration of indigenous fauna and flora is integral to the !Khwa ttu project.

The challenges facing the !Khwa ttu Centre are two-fold. On the one hand, the project has to be financially viable and sustainable. On the other hand, it is vital that the project plays a relevant role in the cultural survival and economic development needs of the remaining 100 000 San people living in southern Africa.

AN INTERNATIONAL PERSPECTIVE

The Griqua National Conference initiated global networking for the Khoe-San, utilising various statutory instruments and agencies of the United Nations. The statutory instruments include, among others, the International Covenant on Civil and Political Rights, which has universal application, and Convention No. 169 of the International Labour Organization (ILO), which has specific application to indigenous people.

The ILO adopted the first comprehensive international instrument setting forth the rights of indigenous and tribal populations in 1957. This Convention was followed, in 1989, by the Indigenous and Tribal Peoples Convention (No. 169). Now part of international law, Convention No. 169 requires ratifying states to:

- adopt special measures for safeguarding the institutions, properties, labour, cultures and environments of indigenous and tribal peoples
- recognise and protect the social, cultural, religious and spiritual values of indigenous and tribal peoples, and to respect their values, practices and institutions
- establish ways and means for indigenous people to develop their own institutions
- acknowledge the right of indigenous people to decide their own priorities for the process of development
- recognise indigenous and tribal peoples' rights of ownership and possession over the lands which they traditionally occupy
- establish adequate procedures within the national legal system to resolve land claims brought by indigenous and tribal peoples.

An important international agency with which the Griqua National Conference networks is the United Nations Working Group on Indigenous Populations (UNWGIP). Established in 1982, it provides an international forum for indigenous and tribal peoples and offers solidarity to members in their attempts to apply pressure on their governments to recognise the rights of indigenous people. In 1993 the Working Group completed the United Nations Draft Declaration on the Rights of Indigenous Peoples. The draft declaration deals with the right to self-determination, self-government and autonomy, land and territorial rights, cultural rights and collective rights. This instrument, although not legally binding, is an important milestone in the recognition of the rights of indigenous people.

With particular regard to Africa, the Griqua National Conference networks with the Indigenous Peoples of Africa Co-ordinating Committee (IPACC). Established in 1996, with headquarters in Cape Town, this advocacy network of Africa-based organisations has over seventy members. Its representatives meet annually during the meeting of UNWGIP in Geneva, Switzerland. In southern Africa, IPACC has played a role in building alliances between Khoekhoe and San groups.

UNITY IN DIVERSITY

Is cultural survival a romantic notion, a hankering for the past in an era of rapid and threatening change? Is cultural survival relevant in today's world? Is it even possible? Ask the English, the Germans, the French, the Greeks, the Italians, the Japanese or any other identifiable national group whether they would be where they are and what they are if their cultures did not survive to the present. They would surely have little alternative but to admit that they are what they are precisely because their cultures did survive and are nurtured every time they speak their own languages, practise their own religions and live according to their own mores, customs and laws. Their confidence, pride and self-esteem come from their history, their knowledge of themselves and the security their national identity gives them.

Why should it be any different for indigenous people who did not have the opportunity, skills and technology to defend their languages, their religious practices and their mores and customs against invaders who were technologically better equipped and thus able to suppress them? Does being dispossessed of one's land and resources and forced to accept the ways of one's oppressors mean that the right to self-expression, self-esteem and group identity should be relinquished? In the context of South Africa, it is too simplistic to say, 'The San and the Khoekhoen were primitive people. Although they were coerced into becoming labourers and had to occupy the lowest levels of colonial society, they were integrated into a socially and economically developed society which was far superior to anything they could have hoped for. By imitating developed societies, they were thus spared the agony of developing their own.' While such a paternalistic statement can be cogently argued in terms of the realities of the time, it disregards the right of indigenous people to freedom – not only the freedom of movement, but also the freedom of choice and the freedom to develop themselves according to their own history, culture and aspirations. For the descendants of the first people of South Africa, this freedom cannot be fully expressed unless they know their history and understand their own culture so that they can determine their own future and articulate it according to their own aspirations.

With the sudden arrival of colonial masters the indigenous people of South Africa were denied the opportunity to follow their own development paths to their own future. The imposition of a foreign culture at the same time as the loss of their traditional resources tossed the indigenous people of southern Africa upon the turbulent seas of rapid social change, leaving them to cling to the flotsam left in the wake of the powerful colonial ship of state as it ploughed relentlessly along its course of exploitation and acquisition. But times have changed. The indigenous people of southern Africa need to reconcile their present with their past so that their future will have the strengthened foundations on which every viable society necessarily has to be built. This is why so many indigenous people's organisations aimed at reconciling Khoe-San identity and heritage have come into being. It is also the reason why cultural survival is not only important but indeed critical to sustainable development. Cultural survival provides the sense of identity, purpose and self-confidence necessary to motivate, drive and sustain the development process.

The constitution of the new South Africa gives statutory recognition to the country's cultural diversity, including its first people. Its architects were well aware that as long as people are made to feel inadequate about their origins and are perceived as culturally and racially inferior, there can be little hope for sustainable peace and development. The vision enshrined in the constitution and symbolised in the coat of arms is of a culturally diverse and vibrant society, one in which mutual understanding, respect, the recognition of individual worth, and an appreciation of the respective contributions made by the country's diverse people are held to be inviolable. It is only when this is achieved that we will fully understand the essential wisdom of !ke e: /xarra //ke, and truly celebrate its promise of unity in diversity.

A BRIEF HISTORY OF THE GRIQUA

In 1740, Adam Kok I (c. 1710–95), believed to have been an emancipated slave, acquired grazing rights in the Piketberg area. By all accounts, Kok was an astute man and a natural leader with considerable foresight. This is demonstrated by the fact that the Chaguriqua, Grigriqua, !Kora and a group of Basters who were living in the area under precarious circumstances were attracted to Kok and looked to him for support. Believed to have been of mixed origins, Kok understood their vulnerability and set about creating a settlement that would provide them with a measure of security. Among his followers were people who possessed horses, wagons and guns and who were fluent in Dutch. Others observed their Khoekhoe origins and spoke, among others, Gri, Grigri and Guri. They were a disparate group, and it is to Kok's considerable credit that he managed to amalgamate them into a single human conglomerate, known as the Griqua, and establish a leadership fountain-head from which has flowed a dynastic order that has continued to the present day.

A typical !Kora settlement on the banks of the Orange River. It is likely that the trading posts established by Cornelis Kok and Barend Barends were similar in style. Note the swimmers using swimming logs. Painting by Samuel Daniell. (MuseumAfrica)

Independence: A prime motivation

Notwithstanding their diverse origins and limited resources, the Griqua refused to succumb to colonial dominance and a life of servitude. However, this was a difficult row to hoe. Even though the VOC recognised Kok as a *kaptyn* (chief), this carried little weight with the white farmers who, in their move up the west coast in search of new land for grazing and cultivation, exerted increasing pressure on Griqua pasture lands. The Griqua chief knew that he and his people would not be able to resist this pressure and so they withdrew from Piketberg and settled further north in the Kamiesberg. However, they were still vulnerable and it was only a matter of time before they had to move again. In preparation, the chief sent his son, Cornelis Kok I (c.1746–1820), to explore the area along the Orange River. There Kok came into contact with various Koranna and Tswana groups and established a number of cattle posts along the river. He also went deep into Transorangia, the territory beyond the Orange River, to trade.

Cornelis Kok I, who by 1795 had become the chief of the Griqua, sent his son, Adam Kok II, and his nephew, Barend Barends, to Klaarwater, where the London Missionary Society had established a mission station. Klaarwater, later renamed Griquatown, grew in size and Adam Kok II and Barend Barends were stationed there permanently as chiefs. Around 1810 Cornelis Kok I relocated from Kamiesberg to Campbell in Transorangia. After his death in 1820, he was succeeded by his son, Cornelis Kok II. In time, Campbell would develop into an independent captaincy.

In Griquatown, dissension among the local population and the influence exerted by the missionaries resulted in the election of Andries Waterboer as Griqua chief. A protégé of the missionaries, Waterboer was also recognised as the official Griqua chief by the Cape government. The increasing role which the missionaries came to play in religious and political matters in Griquatown led to the eventual withdrawal of Barend Barends and Adam Kok II from the chieftaincy. Barends moved to Boetsap, which now formed the third Transorangia captaincy (the others being Griquatown and Campbell). Kok settled in the territory between the Vaal and Riet rivers, which became known as Griqua East.

In 1822 Dr John Philip of the London Missionary Society persuaded Adam Kok II to move to its new mission station, Philippolis. The Philippolis captaincy stretched along the Orange River from Bethulie in the east to Reddersburg in the north and along the Riet River to the Modder River in the west. But the captaincy was unstable, initially because of internal divisions between the different groups of which it was comprised and, after 1825, as a result of the influx of white farmers emigrating from the Cape to escape British rule. The newcomers refused to acknowledge the authority of the Griqua chief, and did not hesitate to appropriate the best fountains and grazing lands. As white settlement in the region increased, Griqua landowners, contrary to the explicit instructions of their chief and in conflict with Griqua common law and custom, began to sell their land to the farmers. The gradual erosion of Griqua authority had begun.

Chief Adam Kok III was a man of great courage and determination who fought for Griqua retention of the Philippolis captaincy. His position became impossible after British betrayal and withdrawal of support. As a result, Kok was left no alternative but to lead his 2 000 followers in an epic trek across present-day Lesotho and the Drakensberg to Nomansland, known today as East Griqualand.

Loss of independence

Adam Kok III (1811–75) became chief of the Philippolis captaincy in 1837. Under his leadership the Griqua negotiated a treaty with the governor, Sir George Napier, in terms of which Griqua independence was recognised. The 1842 treaty also granted ownership of the land lying between the Orange and Modder rivers to the Griqua people. Furthermore, Adam Kok would receive arms, money and protection against white intrusion from the south in return for defending the Cape Colony's Orange River boundary from attack by Bantu-speaking people from the north.

Napier's successor, Sir Peregrine Maitland, had other ideas. He travelled north to Touwfontein where he met Kok and other Griqua leaders to negotiate a new treaty. With this commenced the steady erosion of Griqua rights in the Philippolis captaincy. The rights of white farmers to parts of the captaincy were acknowledged and the captaincy was thus divided into two sections: an 'unleasable' southern section, including Philippolis, whose ownership could not be transferred to whites, and a northern section along the Riet River, which could be leased to British subjects for a period not exceeding forty years. It was also agreed that a British Resident with a small garrison would be stationed at Philippolis to implement the conditions of the treaty. However, when the Resident relocated to Bloemfontein as a result of conflict along the Caledon River, Philippolis and the function of

The steady incursion of white farmers into the Philippolis captaincy was the main reason for its eventual collapse. Painting by Charles Bell. (MuseumAfrica)

Griqua gatekeeping along the Cape Colony's northern borders lost their importance. Philip's ambitious plans for a Griqua captaincy had now become largely irrelevant.

Sir Harry Smith, who became governor of the Cape in 1847, converted the forty-year leases into leases held in perpetuity. He was an impetuous man and, without consulting London, proclaimed British sovereignty over Transorangia, which now became known as the Orange River Sovereignty.

The 1848 annexation was expensive and did not accord with British policy. The British government decided to abandon the Sovereignty and Sir George Clerk was sent from London to negotiate a British withdrawal from the territory. Ignoring both Griqua and Sotho leaders, he entered into direct negotiations with the white farmers, the only group that was not opposed to British withdrawal. Negotiations led to the Bloemfontein Convention of 1854, which paved the way for the establishment of the independent Republic of the Orange Free State on that part of Sovereignty land that was inhabited and administered by whites. Britain's former allies, the Griqua and the Sotho, were abandoned to their fate. At the same time, a verbal agreement was struck between Sir George Clerk, Sir Harry Smith and the representatives of the newly established republic that all Griqua land sold to whites was to pass into the control of the Orange Free State government.

By the mid-1800s a certain measure of prosperity had come to the Philippolis captaincy. Wool farming had been successfully introduced and administration had been improved. By the time the London Missionary Society withdrew in 1855, an independent congregation had become well established at Philippolis. The school and church

Philippolis, named after Dr John Philip of the London Missionary Society, became the capital of the Philippolis captaincy. Painting by Charles Bell. (MuseumAfrica).

were fully functional and both the minister and schoolteacher were Griqua. Twenty-five years after its establishment, the captaincy had the potential of becoming a viable political and administrative entity, but its authority had for too long been eroded by the Boers residing in its territory. And the leaders of the Orange Free State took advantage of this. At first they tried to force the Griqua into a treaty, but it was one-sided and, not surprisingly, the Griqua refused to sign it. The Boers were not deterred. Recalling the Bloemfontein Convention of 1854 and the verbal agreement they had made with Clerk and Smith, the republicans immediately began with arrangements to incorporate the captaincy into the Orange Free State. In 1857 the republic officially appointed its own field-cornets in the Philippolis captaincy and in this way began to exercise its authority within the borders of the captaincy, in open defiance of the Griqua chief.

Unable to obtain protection or even support from the British authorities, it became obvious that Kok and his followers had little alternative but to act on Governor Sir George Grey's suggestion to abandon the Philippolis captaincy. In 1861 the remaining Griqua-owned land in the captaincy was sold to the Republic of the Orange Free State for £4 000. Shortly thereafter, the majority of the Griqua people gathered their belongings and trekked across the Drakensberg to the ominously named Nomansland, later known as East Griqualand.

Life in East Griqualand got off to a difficult start. The Griqua arrived virtually bankrupt, their earlier prosperity wiped out by drought, cattle theft, dealings with dishonest government officials, and accidents on the way to their new home. Starting from scratch, they slowly rebuilt their lives. Gradually, their newly established but impoverished capital began to take shape in the foothills of the Drakensberg and they named it Kokstad after their leader. Despite tremendous odds, the Griqua captaincy survived as an independent polity for some ten years before it was annexed by the Cape government in 1874.

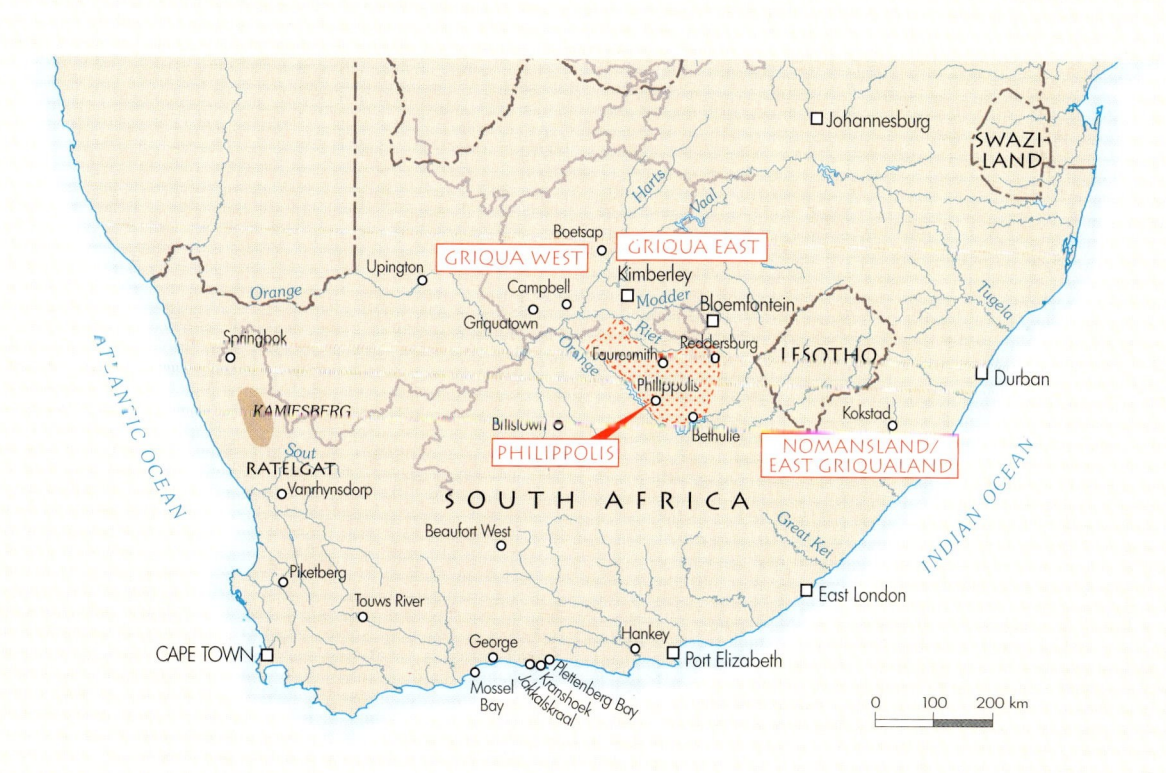

The refusal to live a life of servitude and the desire to be self-sufficient triggered a Griqua diaspora that eventually led to the establishment of the Griqua West, Griqua East, Philippolis and East Griqualand captaincies during the 1800s.

Visionary leadership

Adam Kok III died the following year and there is a lack of clarity over who his successor was. Logically, he should have been succeeded by his younger brother, Adam 'Muis' Kok, but historical records show that there was some doubt about his suitability. Adding to the uncertainty is the prominent role Margriet Kok, the widow of Adam Kok III, played in the leadership affairs of the Griqua and in the 1878 rebellion against the Cape government to reassert Griqua independence. After the death of Adam 'Muis' Kok during the rebellion, the Griqua leadership mantle either remained with or was handed to Margriet Kok.

In 1896, Rachel Susanna Kok, the youngest daughter of Adam 'Muis' Kok, married Andrew Abraham Stockenstrom Le Fleur I (1867–1941). Thus the bloodline of the Kok dynasty passed to the Le Fleur family. The new Griqua chief was the son of Abraham Le Fleur, a former adviser to Adam Kok III and a member of his council. As the relationship between the two families was very close, Le Fleur continued in these capacities when Margriet Kok acted as paramount chief after her husband's death.

The young Le Fleur was a deeply religious man. On 9 May 1889, while on retreat on Manyane Mountain in the Matatiele district, he received a message from God. According to Le Fleur, God instructed him to 'go out and gather the bones of Adam Kok and call the people from the nations so that they can become a People and I can be their God'. That instruction to reunite the Griqua people, with God at the helm, became his mission in life and his inspiration.

As paramount chief, Le Fleur saw the re-establishment of the East Griqualand captaincy as his first task in bringing together the disparate Griqua people. However, the government got wind of his plans and, after a skirmish with colonial forces, Le Fleur was arrested for treason. He was tried by Judge Jones and sentenced on 5 May 1898 to fourteen years' hard labour at the Breakwater Prison in Cape Town. Reflecting on that day when he had to say goodbye to his wife and fourteen-month-old son before being imprisoned in a cold

Andrew Abraham Stockenstrom Le Fleur I (centre) with his supporters outside the Kokstad courthouse. Le Fleur was arrested for treason in 1898 and sentenced to fourteen years' hard labour after attempting to reconstitute the East Griqualand captaincy, which had been annexed by the British in 1874.

cell in Kokstad pending his removal to Cape Town, Le Fleur drew a parallel with the biblical concept of 'being driven into the wilderness'. He viewed his incarceration as part of a process of tempering the steel of his resolve to follow God's commandment given to him on Manyane Mountain.

Not long after being jailed, Le Fleur wrote that God had sent him a vision assuring him that he would be granted an early release. As his dreary life in prison wore on, his faith began to waiver. One day, while driving a crane, he loaded a seven-ton stone and after ensuring that the harness was tightly fastened around the stone, it nevertheless slipped out as he hoisted it up. It came crashing down, smashing a loading wagon right next to him into a mass of twisted steel and splintered wood. For Le Fleur, there could be no doubt as to what this signified. He never again doubted the promise made to him on Manyane Mountain.

When Queen Victoria died on 10 January 1901, Le Fleur felt that he should wait upon God and not make any effort himself to apply for amnesty. His fellow prisoners were amazed at this, but he told

A BRIEF HISTORY OF THE GRIQUA

> **Cornelius de Bruyn – A controversial leader**
>
> *When the Kneg was sentenced to imprisonment in the Breakwater Prison in Cape Town, the Cape government appointed Cornelius George de Bruyn as leader of the Griqua people. Many saw De Bruyn as a government stooge and therefore did not acknowledge his leadership. This left the Griqua in a state of limbo. Some chose to remain in East Griqualand while others followed the Kneg to the Cape. Some of those who moved to the Cape later returned to East Griqualand where they regrouped under the* **Baanbrekersraad van Oos-Griekwaland** *(The Pioneers Council of East Griqualand).*
>
> *As a result of overtures made by the Griqua National Conference of South Africa in pursuance of its drive to reunite the Griqua people, the Baanbrekersraad merged with the Griqua National Conference and an agreement of incorporation was signed on 23 November 1996.*

them his amnesty was part of God's plan for him and that He would reveal the date of his release on 2 January 1903. Immediately after the morning parade on the declared day, Le Fleur informed his fellow convicts that God told him he would be released at 15h00 on Friday, 3 April 1903. He added that on his release he would be saluted by their arrogant and unpopular prison overseer, a prophecy which raised the eyebrows of his incredulous fellow inmates. He wrote of inner doubts, but adhered to God's warning to him not ever to allow Satan to cast doubt on His promises. As the day drew closer, he became increasingly confident and defiant in his spurning of Satan's attacks. This confidence helped to reconfirm his faith and his belief in God's divine purpose for him. On 3 April 1903, to the amazement and awe of his fellow prisoners, Andrew Le Fleur's release from prison was announced. As predicted, he emerged from the Breakwater Prison at precisely 15h00 on the same day, flanked by two senior prison officials. As they walked past the prison overseer, the official had no alternative but to draw himself to attention and salute the trio. It is said that there was a twinkle in Le Fleur's eye as he walked tall through the gateway to freedom.

With the fulfilment of the prophecy of his release, Le Fleur had no further doubt that he had been chosen to be the *Kneg van God* (the Servant of God, a parallel he drew with Moses in Joshua 1:6–7). From then on he was known simply as the *Kneg*, the same name by which he is reverently referred to in the annals of Griqua history. On his release, he was offered a senior government post in the then Rhodesia (Zimbabwe) and a salary of £1 000 per year if he promised to stop organising the Griqua people. However, the Griqua chief and prophet was in no doubt as to where his calling lay.

Banned from returning to Kokstad, he immediately set about uniting the Griqua people on the Cape Flats – much to the disappointment of the Cape authorities. In 1904 he established the Griqua National Conference of South Africa. The name came about as a result of the regular conferences he arranged in different parts of the country

When the Kneg was imprisoned in the Breakwater Prison, he prophesied not only the exact time and date of his early release but also that he would be saluted by his unpopular warder. This photograph shows the re-enactment of the Kneg's release from prison at precisely 15h00 on 3 April 2003 – exactly a hundred years after the actual event.

to gather not only his own followers, but also the majority of self-identified Griqua throughout South Africa. In 1917 he hired a train to bring 800 Griqua followers from Kokstad to Touws River, where he attempted to establish a small-scale agricultural scheme. The project failed because of a lack of infrastructure and government support.

Encouraging self-sufficiency

The *Kneg* strongly advocated the development of agriculture among the Griqua and coloured people. On 27 February 1925 he wrote to the then prime minister, J.B.M. Hertzog, that

> we (must) first lead our people out of the over-crowded state they are living in, on to the Land Settlement [sic]. This is a condition as far as I have travelled, which appeals to our people's satisfaction. They agree it is our only way out, and in this we hope your Government will meet us; meet us as many European Farmers are to-day ready to meet us. That is in letting us have land to plough on even if your Land Board is not prepared to advise the sale of Crown Lands to us, then let it to us; and in that way enable us to pull our people out of the gutter.[11]

Le Fleur understood the importance of land ownership and its capacity to build up capital. He called for the development of a 223 000-acre land scheme along the Orange River, which would provide 'a great opening for the Kimberley and Orange River coloured people, and at £175 000, means about 18/- per Shareholder and would be of the greatest assistance as this estate would build up in 3 years a security worth over half a million.'[12]

In 1923 he founded the Griqua Land Bank, Industries and Development Company (also known as the Griqua Land Bank, Factories and Townships Limited), the purpose of which was to raise capital for the development of agriculture and industries for the benefit of Griqua and coloured people.

Agriculture had the added advantage of helping to create jobs and combat crime, and the *Kneg* pleaded with the government not to squander public money 'in building reformatories for juveniles' but rather to spend it on the development of agricultural schemes.[13] In a letter addressed to both General Jan Smuts and General J.B.M. Hertzog, whose coalition party had come into power in 1934, he again reverted to this theme:

> I give you good advice, give the black man, the brown man, the Griekwa [Griqua] and the poor whites land so that they can earn a living from it and in so doing their children can be kept off the streets. Should you not take my advice you will not be able to keep ahead of the need to build jails.[14]

The *Kneg* made many attempts to get small-scale agricultural projects off the ground. Following the Touws River scheme in 1917, he encouraged unemployed Griqua people in Namaqualand to relocate to Steilhoogte near Klawer where a new agricultural scheme was being developed. Work opportunities included the digging of irrigation canals from the Clanwilliam dam to the lower Olifants River basin. The scheme also held out prospects for the development of sheep farming in the area. In 1924 the Griqua moved again, this time from Steilhoogte to Beeswater near Vredendal. Beeswater was recognised as an official Griqua settlement in 1941.

In 1926, on instruction from the *Kneg*, Griqua people from Cape Town, Kokstad and Touws River relocated to Robberg near Plettenberg Bay. In 1939 they moved to nearby Kranshoek, where the current paramount chief, Andrew Abraham Stockenstrom Le Fleur II, lives and where the headquarters of the Griqua National Conference are situated.

In addition to promoting agriculture and initiating self-help schemes, Le Fleur also started the *Griqua & Coloured People's Opinion* newspaper in 1924, which ran until 1936.

Government authorities viewed the *Kneg* as a political agitator and were suspicious of his ideas, programmes and projects. Indeed, many of his projects were purposely sabotaged. As leader of a nation that had become marginalised, Le Fleur's priority was the development of his people. Even though this concern intersected with the world of politics, the *Kneg* was first and foremost a servant of God. As such, he never intended for the Griqua National Conference to become a political party. Instead, it was established as an inclusive, religion-based organisation, which aspired to promote the welfare of the Griqua through the teachings of the Bible and to empower them through a common group identity and a sense of purpose.

A religious base

The *Kneg* recognised that there was a need to make the teachings of the Bible relevant to life's daily struggles and to do this in a sustainable and supportive way. To this end, he founded the Griqua Choirs in 1919. An inaugural meeting was held in the Maitland Town Hall at which a number of choirs were established. The choirs performed in the streets of Maitland and the Cape Flats to raise funds for Griqua miners who had lost their jobs when the Okiep copper mine was shut down earlier that year. Subsequently, other choirs were formed, and they proved to be effective mechanisms for raising funds and organising the Griqua and coloured people in even the smallest towns and villages. The Griqua Choirs became a powerful means of fulfilling the first part of God's instruction to the *Kneg* on Manyane Mountain: to 'gather the bones of Adam Kok' so that the Griqua can become a nation.

In 1920 Le Fleur established the Griqua Independent Church of South Africa to prepare the Griqua for the fulfilment of the second part of God's instruction to him on Manyane Mountain – the promise that He will be their God. Today, the church forms the cornerstone of the Griqua revival movement. It embraces Christian principles, but has the added responsibility of ensuring that the *Kneg*'s instructions and prophecies received from God and his messages of love, peace and Griqua unity are upheld by church members and are actively propagated within the wider community. The church is the custodian of the spiritual traditions and culture of the Griqua nation and performs the dual functions of promoting and consolidating Griqua community solidarity, as required by the constitution of the Griqua National Conference. Membership of the Griqua Independent Church is based on branch

This memorial was erected at the place where the Kneg had his camp when he lived at Ratelgat. It is here where he predicted that: 'God will turn this desert into a paradise. Ratelgat will become the property of the Griqua people without a cent being spent by them. Tomorrow Ratelgat will supply water to the Cape. Bishops and government leaders will plead in the dust of Ratelgat for relief from the severe depression that will come. God will talk to the Griqua at Ratelgat and bless His People.'[15]

membership of the Griqua National Conference, the ultimate authority responsible for ensuring that Griqua community solidarity is achieved throughout South Africa.

The prophecies

The spiritual authority of the *Kneg* has been reinforced by the fulfilment of many of his prophecies. In the last two decades before his death in 1941, he became more and more ascetic and spent long periods of time on the farm Luiperskop, which he called Ratelgat, north of Vanrhynsdorp. He used this time to communicate with God and to receive His guidance and instructions. Most importantly, it is here where he made known many of his divine revelations and instructions to the Griqua people. Some notable examples include:

- Andrew Abraham Stockenstrom Le Fleur II, the *Kneg*'s grandson, born on 11 May 1923, would become a future paramount chief of the Griqua. He was inaugurated as paramount chief in 1951.
- A railway line would be built between Sishen and Saldanha Bay. What is more, Le Fleur pinpointed the exact location where it would cross the Sout River and described the route it would follow in the vicinity. All these prophecies have been fulfilled in uncanny detail.
- The Griqua would acquire the farm Luiperskop, to be known as Ratelgat, at absolutely no cost to them. Some sixty-six years after this divine revelation, in May 1999, the then Minister of Agriculture and Land Affairs, Derek Hanekom, donated the farm Luiperskop to the Griqua people as a 'symbolic restitution of land'. The farm was bought by the government from a private legal title holder and transferred as a donation to the Griqua Ratelgat Development Trust. It was officially opened by Paramount Chief A.A.S. Le Fleur II on 11 May 2001.

Andrew Abraham Stockenstrom Le Fleur II, grandson of the prophet and chief, the Kneg, *is the present chief of the Griqua nation.*

Right: The Kneg *not only prophesied that a railway line would be built between Sishen and Saldanha Bay, but also where the tracks would be laid and bridges built in the vicinity of Sout River near Ratelgat.*

A BRIEF HISTORY OF THE GRIQUA

Towards the end of his life, the Kneg moved to Jakkalskraal, a privately-owned farm near Kranshoek, where he died in 1941. The Kneg only rented the house in this picture, but he predicted that one day the Griqua would own the entire farm. His vision was realised when Jakkalskraal was officially handed over to the Griqua nation on 19 November 2001. Profits from the farm, which now has one of the biggest dairy herds in the Plettenberg Bay area, will be used for community development work at Kranshoek.

- The Griqua would acquire the farm, Jakkalskraal, which would become their 'breadbasket during times of hunger'. Jakkalskraal, situated along the Piesang River some eight kilometres from Plettenberg Bay and two kilometres from Kranshoek, was purchased in 1986 by Lanok, a Cape-based parastatal rural development corporation. It was bought on behalf of the Kranshoek community and a dairy was established on the farm. In November 2001 the title-deeds to the farm were officially handed over to Paramount Chief A.A.S. Le Fleur II.
- The Griqua would be represented in Geneva. Between 24 and 28 July 1995 a mandated representative of the Griqua National Conference attended the thirteenth session of the United Nations Working Group on Indigenous Populations held in Geneva. Today, a Griqua representative participates in an official delegation to the Indigenous Peoples of

97

Africa Co-ordinating Committee, an advocacy network of indigenous peoples' organisations in Africa, which meets annually in Geneva as part of the United Nations Working Group on Indigenous Populations.

Not all of Le Fleur's many prophecies have been fulfilled. What is important, however, is that a considerable number of the prophecies that were relevant to the Griqua have come to pass in the way he said they would. The accuracy of his predictions and his spiritual vision have made Le Fleur a powerful source of inspiration and motivation for the Griqua people, both during his lifetime and after his death in 1941. The fulfilment of the *Kneg*'s prophecies over time has served to reinforce the Griqua's faith in God's instruction, given through the *Kneg*, to unite as a nation and to be guided by Him. The Griqua people believe that, as with past revelations, those prophecies that remain to be fulfilled will refresh the spiritual fountain that sustains Griqua unity and national purpose.

The flag of the Griqua National Conference of South Africa. The red panel represents the blood of Christ and the white panel denotes peace. The blue panel signifies the colour of heaven and virtuous living. The dark-green vertical panel symbolises productive and constructive living. In its centre is an image of the kanniedood *aloe (Aloe variegata), known for its tenacity and ability to survive in adverse conditions.*

The Kneg's *grave near Robberg Peninsula in the Plettenberg Bay area is a holy site for the Griqua. People from all over the country meet here on 31 December each year to thank God for the past year and to pray for His guidance and help in the year to come. Here members of the personal choir of the present paramount chief pay tribute to the memory of the Kneg.*

Celebrating Griqua identity

The Griqua celebrate their unity and distinct identity through the use of their own symbols. These comprise a number of heritage sites, traditional dress and culture, a Griqua flag and a Griqua anthem, *God Ewig Groot en Goed* (God Eternal, Great and Good), sung in Afrikaans. Significant events in Griqua history are commemorated with eight special *volksdae* (people's days). These are:

- **10 March**: The birthday of Paramount Chief Abraham Andrew Le Fleur, the son of the *Kneg*, born in 1897.
- **3 April (Breakwater Day)**: Celebration of the *Kneg*'s release from the Breakwater Prison in 1903.
- **6 April**: Founding of the Griqua Independent Church in 1920.
- **11 May (Ratelgat Day)**: Celebration of the official opening of the Ratelgat Development Trust Project in 2001 and the birthday of the present paramount chief, A.A.S. Le Fleur II, born in 1923.

- **2 July (Founder's Day)**: The birthday of Paramount Chief Andrew Abraham Stockenstrom Le Fleur I (the *Kneg*), born in 1867.
- **10 September (Monument Day)**: Celebration of the unveiling of a monument in honour of the early Griqua pioneers at Kranshoek in 1942.
- **14 October (Mother's Day)**: The birthday of Rachel Susanna Le Fleur (née Kok), the *Kneg*'s wife, born in 1878.
- **31 December (Year's Closure)**: The annual gathering at Kranshoek to thank God for his protection of the Griqua during the past year and to ask Him for protection, guidance and prosperity in the year about to begin.

Although the Griqua are a minority group in South Africa, they nevertheless constitute a unique part of the country's human kaleidoscope. The roots of the Griqua are laid down in indigenous soils and their growth has been stimulated by a history of bringing together people of multi-ethnic origins and moulding them into a united community. They have endured dislocation and a diaspora, the consequences of a process of colonisation in which the Griqua were first treated as allies and then came to be seen as expendable. The Griqua were encouraged to invest in Nomansland, a convenient carpet under which they could be swept by a government that was more concerned with the politics of power in southern Africa than in Griqua human rights. However, they came out from under that carpet and today they are a proud and independent people. In recent years the Griqua have called for United Nations protection and recognition of their status as a first nation in South Africa and have demanded full indigenous rights as described in United Nations Resolution 48/163, which launched the International Decade of the World's Indigenous Peoples. They continue to demand due and equal recognition of their distinct cultural identity, cultural objectives, traditional leadership structures and full human rights as enshrined in the new South African constitution, as well as the restitution of land owned by their forebears.

This monument was erected in 1942 at Kranshoek, the headquarters of the Griqua National Conference of South Africa, to commemorate all Griqua pioneers.

NOTES

CHAPTER 1
1. H.J. Deacon and J. Deacon, *Human Beginnings in South Africa* (Cape Town, David Philip, 1999), pp. 5–6.
2. Ibid., p. 77.
3. Ibid., p. 84.
4. Ibid., p. 101.
5. Ibid.
6. Ibid., p. 102.

CHAPTER 2
1. P.V. Tobias, 'Myths and misunderstandings about Khoisan identities and status' in A. Bank (ed.), *The Khoisan Identities and Cultural Heritage Conference* (Cape Town, Institute for Historical Research, University of the Western Cape, 1997), p. 20.
2. D. Sleigh, *The Forts of the Liesbeeck Frontier* (Cape Town, Castle Military Museum, 1996), p. 57.
3. D. Chidester, 'Mutilating meaning: European interpretations of Khoisan languages of the body' in P. Skotnes (ed.), *MISCAST. Negotiating the Presence of the Bushmen* (Cape Town, University of Cape Town Press, 1996), p. 24.
4. Tobias, 'Myths and misunderstandings', p. 20.
5. Ibid.
6. H.J. Deacon and J. Deacon, *Human Beginnings in South Africa: Uncovering the Secrets of the Stone Age* (Cape Town, David Philip, 1999), p. 130.
7. I. Schapera, *The Khoisan Peoples of South Africa* (London, Routledge & Kegan Paul Ltd., 1951), p. 77.
8. Deacon and Deacon, *Human Beginnings*, p. 132.
9. Ibid.
10. N.G. Penn, '"Fated to perish": The destruction of the Cape San' in P. Skotnes (ed.), *MISCAST. Negotiating the Presence of the Bushmen* (Cape Town, University of Cape Town Press, 1996), p. 88.
11. J.S. Marais, *The Cape Coloured People 1652–1937* (Johannesburg, Witwatersrand University Press, 1968), p. 15.
12. P. Skotnes (ed.), *MISCAST. Negotiating the Presence of the Bushmen* (Cape Town, University of Cape Town Press, 1996), pp. 15 and 61.
13. Penn, 'Fated to perish', p. 89.
14. H. Lichtenstein, *Travels in Southern Africa in the Years 1803, 1804, 1805 and 1806* (2 vols., Cape Town, Van Riebeeck Society, 1928–30), vol. I, pp. 217–9.
15. For an explanation of the origin of the term 'Bastaard', see page 55.
16. Marais, *Cape Coloured People*, p. 19.
17. Ibid.
18. G. Theal (ed.), *Records of the Cape Colony* (36 vols., Cape Town, Government of the Cape Colony, 1897–1905), vol. VII, pp. 35–6, quoted in Marais, *Cape Coloured People*, p. 18.
19. G. Thompson, *Travels and Adventures in Southern Africa* (London, Colburn, 1827), pp. 395–8.
20. Marais, *Cape Coloured People*, p. 18.
21. Penn, 'Fated to perish', p. 89.
22. Ibid.
23. Ibid., p. 81.
24. Marais, *Cape Coloured People*, p. 20.
25. Ibid.
26. Ibid.
27. Ibid., p. 22.
28. Ibid., p. 27.
29. Anthing's report reproduced in Skotnes (ed.), *MISCAST*, p. 162.
30. Ibid., p. 174.

CHAPTER 3

1. P. Jolly, 'Between the lines: Some remarks on "Bushman"' in P. Skotnes (ed.), *MISCAST. Negotiating the Presence of the Bushmen* (Cape Town, University of Cape Town Press, 1996), p. 198.
2. J.L. Newman, *The Peopling of Africa* (New Haven and London, Yale University Press, 1995), p. 165.
3. G.M. Theal, *History of Africa South of the Zambesi from 1505 to 1795*, 3rd edn (3 vols., London, Allen & Unwin, 1916–22); G.W. Stow, *The Native Races of South Africa: A History of the Intrusion of the Hottentot and Bantu into the Hunting Grounds of the Bushmen, the Aborigines of the Country* (Swan Sonnenschein, London, 1905).
4. C. Ehret, 'The first spread of food production to southern Africa' in C. Ehret and M. Posnansky (eds.), *The Archaeological and Linguistic Reconstruction of African History* (Berkeley, University of California Press, 1982), pp. 158–81; R. Elphick, *Khoikhoi and the Founding of White South Africa* (Ravan Press, Johannesburg, 1985).
5. A. Smith, 'Khoi/San relationships: Marginal differences or ethnicity?' in P. Skotnes (ed.), *MISCAST. Negotiating the Presence of the Bushmen* (Cape Town, University of Cape Town Press, 1996), p. 250.
6. P. Davison and G. Klinghardt, 'Museum practice, material culture and the politics of identity' in P. McAllister (ed.), *Culture and the Commonplace: Anthropological Essays in Honour of David Hammond-Tooke* (Johannesburg, Wits University Press, 1997), p. 187.
7. Ibid., p. 190.
8. Patricia de Lille, MP, quoted in the *Cape Times*, 30 November 2001.
9. Zackie Achmat, quoted in the *Cape Times*, 30 November 2001.
10. Piet Westra, quoted in the *Cape Times*, 12 December 2001.
11. Quoted in E. Boonzaier, P. Berens, C. Malherbe and A. Smith, *The Cape Herders* (Cape Town and Johannesburg, David Philip, and Ohio University Press, Athens, 1996), p. 63.
12. J. Cope, *The King of the Hottentots* (Cape Town, Howard Timmins, Cape Town, 1967), pp. 77–80 and 92.
13. H.B. Thom (ed.), *Journal of Jan van Riebeeck* (3 vols., Cape Town and Amsterdam, Balkema, 1952), vol. III, pp. 23–5.
14. R. Ross, *Cape of Torments: Slavery and Resistance in South Africa* (London, Routledge & Kegan Paul Ltd., 1983), p. 44.
15. F. Valentijn, *Description of the Cape of Good Hope*, ed. E.H. Raidt, trans. R. Raven-Hart (2 vols., Cape Town, Van Riebeeck Society, 1973), vol. I, p. 219.
16. J.S. Marais, *The Cape Coloured People 1652–1937* (Johannesburg, Witwatersrand University Press, 1968), p. 116.
17. From the very beginning most settlers looked upon the Khoekhoen as being utterly contemptible and as 'creatures' who existed outside their frame of reference and concern and were expendable. See I.D. MacCrone, *Race Attitudes in South Africa – Historical, Experimental and Psychological Studies* (Johannesburg, University of the Witwatersrand Press, 1957), pp. 44–9; Z. Magubane, 'Labour laws and stereotypes: Images of the Khoikhoi in the Cape in the age of abolition', *South African Historical Journal* 35 (1996), pp. 115–34.
18. Z. Magubane, 'Labour laws and stereotypes', p. 117.
19. W. Colebrooke, *Report upon the State of the Hottentots and Bushmen of the Cape of Good Hope* (Cape Town, 1829), p. 20 in Z. Magubane, 'Labour laws and stereotypes', p. 117.
20. R. Ross, *Cape of Torments*, p. 52.
21. Marais, *Cape Coloured People*, p. 157.

CHAPTER 4

1. J.S. Marais, *The Cape Coloured People 1652–1937* (Johannesburg, Witwatersrand University Press, 1968), p. 200.
2. W.M. MacMillan, *The Cape Colour Question* (London, Faber & Gwyer, 1927), p. 256.
3. Ibid., p. 262.
4. *British Parliamentary Papers* [1636] of 1853, p. 25.
5. Marais, *Cape Coloured People*, p. 208.
6. L.M. Thompson, *The Cape Coloured Franchise* (Johannesburg, South African Institute of Race Relations, 1950), p. 8.
7. *Minutes of the Proceedings with Annexures (Selected) of the South African National Convention* (Cape Town, Government Printer, 1911), para. 9.23.
8. Ibid.
9. Ibid.
10. Ibid.
11. *Cape Times*, 14 November 1925.
12. D.F. Malan, *Die Groot Vlug* (Cape Town, The National Party, 1923), p. 12.
13. Ibid.
14. House of Assembly, *Hansard*, Col. 986 (1931).
15. Malan, *Die Groot Vlug*, p. 12.

CHAPTER 5

1. A. Morris, 'Trophy skulls, museums and the San' in P. Skotnes (ed.), *MISCAST. Negotiating the Presence of the Bushmen* (Cape Town, University of Cape Town Press, 1996), p. 67.
2. P.V. Tobias, 'Myths and misunderstandings about Khoisan identities and status' in A. Bank (ed.), *The Khoisan Identities and Cultural Heritage Conference* (Cape Town, Institute for Historical Research, University of the Western Cape, 1997), p. 22.
3. Ibid.
4. Ibid.
5. S. Mguni, 'Unity in diversity', *Sawubona*, September 2002, p. 14.
6. Tobias, 'Myths and misunderstandings', p. 22.
7. *Griqua & Coloured People's Opinion*, New Series No. 1/97, (March 1997), p. 19.
8. A. Morris, 'The Griqua and the Khoikhoi: Biology, ethnicity and the construction of identity' in A. Bank (ed.), *The Khoisan Identities and Cultural Heritage Conference* (Cape Town, Institute for Historical Research, University of the Western Cape, 1997), p. 371.
9. Ibid.
10. Ibid.
11. A.A.S. Le Fleur I, personal communication, 27 February 1925 [Correspondence in the possession of the Griqua National Conference of South Africa].
12. A.A.S. Le Fleur I, Memoir reproduced at Ratelgat, Vredendal, 2 April 1935 [Document in the possession of the Griqua National Conference of South Africa].
13. *Griqua & Coloured People's Opinion*, 2 February 1925.
14. Griqua National Conference of South Africa, Official document produced for the official opening of Ratelgat on 12 May 2001, p. 7.
15. Ibid.